"In the tradition of James Still's R and *The Wolfpen Notebooks*, Judith the talk of her neighbors for thirty five years. From beauty tips to weather predictions, from dream interpretation to home remedies, Hensley's *Mountain Wisdom: Mountain Folk, Volume 1* is a taxonomy of Southern Appalachian ways. Her work as an oral historian, folkways gleaner, and photographer is richly and lovingly organized for readers young and old. Here we can find and enjoy expressions of speech, practical advice, mythology, and guessing games all contained in this unique and welcome volume."

—Marianne Worthington, Poetry Editor,
Now & Then: The Appalachian Magazine

"Judith Victoria Hensley has given us a great gift with her latest book, *Mountain Wisdom: Mountain Folk, Volume 1*. While these pages are filled with sage advice for everyday living, they also help to preserve an endangered cultural tradition. This book has a special spot on my reference shelf."

—Jason Howard, co-author of *Something's Rising*
and editor of *We All Live Downstream*

"Every culture around the world is seeped with customs, traditions, beliefs, and superstitions. Although many resonate with familiarity from place to place, there are those that are truly unique and set apart in certain regions. In *Mountain Wisdom: Mountain Folk, Volume 1*, Ms. Hensley captured a distinct flavor of the mountainous regions of the Southeastern United States. Peculiar, entertaining, and at times humorous, this book is an interesting read."

—Barry Shainbaum, International photographer, speaker, author, and
radio talk show host. Barry Shainbaum Productions of Toronto,
Ontario, Canada

"Readers will find this collection of homey anecdotes and remedies curious, amusing, and familiar. Indeed, the collected wisdom in this book may prompt you to take a different look at a situation or try out a new approach when faced with life's little dilemmas."

—Sky Marietta, Instructor, Harvard Graduate
School of Education; M.A.T., Ed.M.

"Much like my dear granny, a kind soul who saves every scrap of fabric she ever comes across to make colorful and comforting quilts for her children, grandchildren, and great grandchildren, Judith Hensley has spent decades tucking away countless snippets of folk speech and uncommon sayings in the Appalachian mountains in drawers, notebooks, and in the back of her mind in hopes of have an opportunity to share them with others. Decades in the making, this book is Ms. Hensley's masterpiece to date. It is colorful and inviting, but also well-researched and tirelessly crafted into a book that should be handed down to future generations. *Mountain Wisdom: Mountain Folk, Volume 1* offers a colorful and comforting glimpse into the rich culture of mountain folk in the southeastern United States."

> —Cassie M. Robinson Pfleger, 2010 Conference Program Chairperson of the Appalachian Studies Association; Dahlonega, Georgia

"A delightful read overflowing with the wit and wisdom of mountain lore. Ms. Hensley's intimate understanding of Appalachia along with her deep abiding love of its people, heritage and customs inspires each and every page. Read and heed! Within you will discover a wellspring of uncommon knowledge and you will be wiser of mind and richer in spirit . . . "

> —Larry LaFollette, archivist for Southeast Kentucky Community and Technical College and President of the Harlan County Historical Society

"Judy Hensley's collection of mountain lore and wisdom is illustrative of her keen ear and vigor of mountain culture."

> —Roy Silver, Ph. D. Professor of Sociology, Southeast Kentucky Community & Technical College

MOUNTAIN WISDOM
Mountain Folk
Volume 1

Judith V. Hensley

Little Creek Books

A division of Mountain Girl Press
Bristol, VA

Little Creek Books

A division of Mountain Girl Press
Bristol, VA

MOUNTAIN WISDOM: *Mountain Folk, Volume 1*

Published 2010

All quotes and bits of wisdom in this book were recorded over the last thirty-six years from listening to people's conversations in areas of the Southeastern United States including: Kentucky, Tennessee, Virginia, West Virginia, North Carolina, South Carolina, and Georgia. All information is written purely to record the thoughts, speech, wisdom, and culture of the area. Occasionally there may appear several variations of the same thought, recorded as it was heard. Similarities to other collections are purely coincidental. The content is based entirely on what has been heard and recorded by the author. The Home Remedies are not recommended or endorsed by the author in lieu of a physician's care.

You may contact the publisher at:
Little Creek Books
c/o Mountain Girl Press
2195 Euclid Avenue, Suite 7
Bristol, VA 24201-3655
Email: publisher@littlecreekbooks.com

Cover design by Carlson ProType.
Pictured are Wick and Florence Hamlin with daughters Marie and Gracie (the two oldest children of sixteen). The dog, Old Watch, rescued Wick from a wild boar attack while he was hunting on Brush Mountain in Harlan, Kentucky. Wick and Florence are the grandparents of author, Judith Victoria Hensley.

ISBN: 978-0-9843192-7-5

Table of Contents

A Letter From the Author

I was born in Harlan County, Kentucky, but grew up in a suburban area outside of Chicago, Illinois. At that time, Chicago was known as the "melting pot" of the world. Irish, Italian, Polish, German, Scandinavian, Oriental, African American, Appalachian, and many other cultures were represented in the area where we lived. It was because of the differences and similarities in these cultures that made me wonder about my own heritage from the mountains of Kentucky.

My love affair for the mountains and the region known as Appalachia came early in my life. Riding down the Interstate 75 corridor with my dad at the wheel, I always felt like we were heading for heaven on earth. The beauty of the mountains, the loving and generous spirits of the people, the spirituality of the place, and the vast sense of freedom that I felt only in the mountains drew me to this place beyond reason. Relatives often told me I was born in the wrong time and the wrong place . . . that I had the heart of a pioneer, an explorer, a settler. I don't know about that, but I certainly was enchanted with the romantic notions I held about the place.

At an early age I learned to listen, to interpret accents, and to understand meanings of peculiar phrases. As an adult, I began to realize the uniqueness of the Appalachian culture and value the humor, imagery, and poetry of the language. A true Appalachian will use a simile, metaphor, or idiom in daily conversation to express the most mundane or common thoughts just to spice up the flow of conversation without planning or forethought. I catch myself using this pattern of speech daily, and am sorry for those who feel that they have "outgrown" the region, the speech, or their roots.

There is a wonderful line from one of my favorite movies, *A Walk in the Clouds,* when Alberto Aragon says, "Just because I speak with an accent does not mean I think with an accent."

Folk wisdom, stories, values, and attitudes also became a focus of what I wanted to discover about my people and what I hoped to help preserve. I had the privilege of stepping in and out of the 18th, 19th, and 20th century lifestyles as I grew up and visited many isolated areas in Appalachia. Early in my life I was amazed that nestled in the hills and hollows, there were pockets of people who had changed little since the late 1800s and early 1900s, co-existing with the culture of 20th century America, although almost none still remain to date.

My first official notes about Appalachian language were for an Appalachian Studies class at Cumberland College in Williamsburg, Kentucky in 1974. My stack of notes has grown slowly over the years. It occurred to me that should something happen to me, all those years of notes on envelopes, notepads, store receipts, and napkins would look like trash to anyone who came across them and would end up in the garbage. It seemed prudent to organize those notes and get them in print for whoever might be interested. I never dreamed my collection of scribbling through the years would take two or three volumes to contain them! Almost every day I hear more interesting things to record.

I did not set out to gather this body of information for the purpose of scholarly evaluation, but rather as an effort to preserve the beauty of a language and people that are gradually becoming homogenized into the larger scope of mainstream American society. Their wisdom and understanding of their world should not perish without an attempt to preserve as much as possible.

There are other more academic endeavors, I am sure, but mine has been a labor of love.

Simply by listening and recording, I have attempted to document the sound and flow of this section of Appalachia, the values, beliefs, and thought processes expressed in everyday language through a cross section of ages, vocations, gender, and communities. Changes creep into any culture slowly but surely. It is my desire to preserve things that are in place at this point in time in my place. Every day I hear or say some unique phrase that I realize I don't have included in this body of work. I've added many even in the last days of proofreading, but this work could go on for many more years. It finally was time for me to stop and hope that someone else will continue to record what they hear.

The following excerpts are from a journal I kept in college. The first date is January 23, 1979.

Appalachia,

Land of my fathers, and my fathers' fathers — how could anyone misunderstand you so? How could they abuse and betray you so unknowingly? It is that they need to feel superior to someone, so they wind up picking you as a target? Or are they genuinely concerned with your well-being, and try so hard to help and understand you that they smother you in the process? I'd like to believe the best, but sometimes, I just don't know.

Appalachia, can you ever forgive them?

My Appalachia

The distant call of whip-or-wills
Echoes faintly o'er the hills,
Ringing out the mountains' songs
of those who love and who belong.
'Tis yesterday's song and shadows cast
Memories of a misty past . . .
Of people proud, and strong, and free,
People oft' forgotten by history.
If you could speak to me, what would you say?
What forgotten stories have passed your way?
What secrets are sealed within your folds;
Stories of women and men of old?

J.V.H. 1979
Appalachian Studies Class — Cumberland College
Williamsburg, KY

Acknowledgments

Thank you:

To everyone who contributed their favorite bits of mountain wisdom and traditional information to this collection;

To the Foxfire Museum and staff who have always supported student work and my work in the region;

To all those who value this region and consider its culture worthy of preserving;

To Susan and Carrie Noe, Gladys Hensley, Bud Fultz, and Jeremy Bryson for proofreading;

To everyone who allowed me to use photographs from their personal collections and especially the following people who dragged out family albums:

Danny and Ettafaye (Hensley) Bruce
Bill and Sarah (Boggs) Conatser
Jean Correll
Justin and Betty (Blevins) Curry
Bud Fultz
Ernest and Gladys (Hamlin) Hensley
Sam Hensley
The Late Opal Hopkins
Elizabeth Howard

Fred Howard
Darla Jackson
Esther Fowler LeClaire
Jeanette McDaniels
Gail Owens
Rhonda Robinson
Roxie Rowland
Cheryl Sargent
Marion and Wilma Wilson

Author photo on back cover by Rhonda Long Robinson

DISCLAIMER:

At no time or under any circumstances does the author of this work support, endorse, or recommend any of the home remedies in lieu of being treated by a personal physician. The information on these pages is solely for the purpose of recording what others may hold as true or real.

All information is recorded simply as documentation of what has been said or recommended by others in an effort to capture the poetry, imagery, idioms, similes, metaphors, humor, sarcasm, and bits of wisdom from the region. Any resemblance to other works of a similar nature is purely coincidental.

Dedication

To my parents, Ernest and Gladys Hensley, the Ashers, Daniels, the Hamlins, Hensleys, Lees, Smiths, Saylors, Scotts, Wilsons and all of the related clans — my aunts, uncles, and cousins who have scattered far from their mountain roots but who will always have highland blood in their veins.

To my friends and acquaintances who have let me listen, helped me listen, and who have given me notes to enrich the content of this collection.

Ernest and Gladys Hensley

Beauty Tips and Good Grooming

Patricia Blanton

Beauty is a virtue held in highest esteem among mountain folk, although their definition of beauty goes beyond the superficial to include moral character and personality. A clear complexion, shiny hair, bright eyes, and a shapely figure have always been admired and valued.

1

beauty

- If you want to be beautiful, get up at daybreak and wash your face in the morning dew.
- On the first day of May, rub May apple juice on your face and skin, if you want to be beautiful the rest of the year.

blush

- For a natural blush, use the crushed blooms from the huckleberry bush.

complexion

- If you wash your face with lye soap at least twice a day, you will have a clear, glowing complexion.
- Always wash your face in cold water to keep pores tight.
- Wash your face with warm soapy water and a rough wash cloth followed by a rinse in cold water to keep a clear complexion.
- You can put natural clay on your face and let it dry, then wash it off for a clear complexion.
- Mix honey and warm water to a very thin consistency. Spread it over the face and neck and leave it for a few minutes, then wash off with a warm, rough washcloth and rinse thoroughly.
- A light rinse with vinegar water (1 teaspoon of vinegar to one cup of warm water) will help keep a clear complexion.

eyes

- To take swelling out of your eyes and make them look less puffy, lay cucumber slices on your eyelids and rest for 10 minutes.
- When you remove tea bags from your cup, let them cool and place one on each eye while you rest for ten minutes to take out any puffiness and make eyes look brighter.
- Place dry tea bags on the eyes to draw out puffiness.

fingernails

- Soak fingertips in jello for fast growing, beautiful fingernails.
- To break a habit of biting nails, put quinine underneath the fingernails.

- To stop yourself from biting your nails, put hot pepper juice under your fingernails.

hair

- If you would like to have natural looking highlighted streaks in your hair, mix lemon juice and vinegar and comb it through your hair before going out into the sunshine.
- For gray hair, rub walnut juice into the hair, especially where graying begins at the temple.
- Put water out of a grapevine on your hair to make it curly.
- If you would really like to have shiny hair, rinse it in beer.
- Every once in a while, wash your hair in soap powder if you want it to really shine.
- Mix lemon juice and vinegar and soak your hair in it if you want to lighten your hair all over.
- If you want really healthy hair, apply mayonnaise to your hair and wrap it in a damp, hot towel for an hour before shampooing.
- Mix beer and egg together to make a hair conditioner that is healthy for your hair and will also give it a pretty shine. You put it on your hair after shampooing and leave it in for 3–5 minutes before rinsing. Make sure you rinse thoroughly!
- Put a little baking soda in your hair as you wash it to give it a good shine.
- Rinsing your hair in vinegar water after a shampoo will give it a good shine.
- If you get chewing gum in your hair, you can get it out by applying mayonnaise or peanut butter or mustard on the gum. It will let the gum slip down the hair shafts without having to cut it out.
- Occasionally, rub extra virgin olive oil through your hair. Wrap your hair in a warm/hot towel and let it set for an hour. Shampoo and rinse thoroughly.
- Add vinegar to your shampoo to help strip it of any kind of build up from your water. It will keep your hair healthy and make it shine.

hands

- To remove the smell of onion from the hands, you can rub your hands with a spoon under running water.
- Rub a fresh slice of lemon over your hands after cutting onions to remove the smell.
- Rub lemon rind over smelly hands to remove the scent.
- After cutting onions, rub a slice of fresh tomato over the hands. The onion scent will vanish.

lips

- To give your lips a nice shine all the time without using lipstick, rub a little Vaseline on them.
- To keep lips soft and uncracked, rub Vaseline on them before you go to bed at night and before you go out in freezing weather.

perfume

- If you are out of perfume, you can put a dab of pure vanilla extract behind your ears and on your pulse points for a nice clean, sweet smell.
- Freshly crushed rose petals or crushed violets will produce a light pleasant scent when rubbed on pulse points.

photographs

- If you want to take a pretty picture, put Vaseline on your eyelids and lips.
- Place a small dot of black in the corner of each eye to give them distinction in a black and white photograph.
- Place Vaseline on your lips to give a pretty, natural shine.
- In a black and white photograph, a light coating of blackberry juice or cherry juice will give the lips a natural looking distinction.
- A dab of uncooked lard on the lips will add a nice shine for a photograph.

shoes

- If you are out of shoe polish, use a little lard to give your shoes a real shine.

skin

- To get a really dark tan, mix iodine and motor oil together and use it for tanning oil.
- Mix brown shoe polish and any good brand of body lotion together and apply it to your legs to make them look like you have a natural tan. (Cheerleaders use to do this trick to make their legs look nice in the winter.)

scenting garments pleasantly

- Dry wild roses and put them in a hope chest or in a bureau drawer to scent the contents with a nice smell.
- If you make a closet out of cedar, you will never have to worry about moths getting in your clothes and the scent of clothes stored there will be woodsy and pleasant.

washing

- Pick up a wet dishrag and wipe a child's face with it to insure that they will grow up to be beautiful.
- Wash your face at least twice a day.
- Wash your body at least once a day.
- Wash your hands often.
- Bathe at least once a week.

Bob Cawood, Will Bailey,
Carlo Jones, Jerome Howard
Harlan, KY

5

~ **Dreams** ~

Nancy Conatser
Marshes Siding, KY

Dreams have long been regarded as a link between the real world and a spiritual world. Sometimes they bring joy, comfort, warning, or maybe even confusion. Since ancient times people have sought to give meaning and validation to dreams.

Mountain folk look for the obvious meanings in dreams and sometimes throw in a bit of superstition to make their interpretations clear.

A

acorns

- If you dream of planting acorns, a long term venture will be successful.
- If you dream of planting an acorn and see the worms eat it up, or a squirrel come and carry it away, it is a warning that a long term venture will fail.
- If a woman dreams of eating acorns it means that she will be successful in her life.
- If you dream of shaking acorns from a tree represents something you want very badly. If many acorns fall, you will be blessed with what you want. If you can't shake any loose, you will not get the thing you desire.

almonds

- If you dream of eating almonds and they taste sweet, all will be well.
- If you dream of eating almonds and they taste bitter so that you have to spit them out, it is a warning to change any plans you have for the immediate future.

angels

- If you dream that an angel is with you, guiding you somewhere to safety, it means that you are facing bad times, but you will come through fine.
- If you dream of the death angel two times, on the third time, he will come to take you.
- If you dream of what looks like a person hovering, or floating in the air with no feet, they are an angel.
- If an angel appears to you in a dream and gives you a specific message, pay close attention. You must remember the message and act accordingly when you wake up.
- If an angel comes to you in a dream and gives you an answer or a solution to a problem you are having, the angel has carried the answer to your prayers for you.
- To dream of an angel is good luck.

animal

- If you dream of any kind of black animal chasing you, like a panther, or a bear, it is something you fear. If you dream it more than once, make yourself turn around in the dream and face the animal. It will disappear and so will your fear.
- If you dream of an animal speaking to you, take heed of the message.

B

baby

- If you dream of holding a happy baby, all will go well in this period of your life.
- If you dream of trying to comfort a fussy baby to no avail, there is trouble or sorrow ahead in this period of your life.
- If a woman dreams of nursing a baby at her breast, someone very close to her will deceive her or break her heart.

bear

- Being chased by a bear in a dream represents a fear you have of something. That fear has power over you. Look at other people in the dream, how they behave, and the place you go for refuge.
- If you dream of killing a bear, you will overcome fears or difficulties.

bed

- To dream of being in a comfortable bed means your life will be comfortable for a season.
- To dream of an uncomfortable bed means your life is going to be troublesome in the days ahead.
- To dream of a clean, white bed that has not been slept in, but is waiting for you indicates joy and blessings ahead.

bird

- If you dream of a bird in your house, death is at your door.
- If you dream of a bird staring at you, it is trying to tell you something. Listen.

- If you dream of singing birds, it is a sign of happiness coming to you.
- If you dream of flying birds, it is a good omen.
- If you dream of blackbirds, beware.
- If you dream of killing a bird, you are about to make a serious mistake in your life. Reconsider your choices and take another path.

birth

- If you dream of a birth, it is a sign of death.
- If you dream of a stillbirth, one of your dreams that you hold dear will die.

blood

- If you dream of blood, someone is going to die.
- If you dream of blood on your clothes, a rumor or the truth will bring public shame to you.

butterfly

- To dream of a butterfly landing on you signifies blessings in the near future.
- To dream of a butterfly (or butterflies) among living flowers means happiness in your life.
- If you dream of a butterfly among dead flowers or dying weeds and the butterfly does not land, you have trouble ahead.

C

candles

- To dream of candles burning steadily means that there is nothing you need to fear about the future.
- If you dream of candles that go out or are snuffed out, it means a time of fear and worry head.

cats

- If you dream of a black cat following you, you have a secret enemy.
- If you dream of cats playing or coming to you, it is a sign of good luck.

- If you dream of a cat purring while sitting in your lap or laying on you, it means you are in a season of peace.
- If you dream of being attacked by a cat, you have an enemy afoot.
- It is good luck to dream of a gray cat.

circle

- If you find a circle or ring of mushrooms growing wild, it is called a fairy ring or a wishing ring. Stand inside the circle and make a wish, but you cannot tell where the circle is. If you do, your wish won't come true.

Mary Eva Vance Curry
Harlan County, KY

crow

- If you dream of a crow sitting on a doorpost, it is a sign of death in that house.
- If a crow speaks to you in a dream, what it says will be deceitful.

crown

- If you dream of having a crown placed on your head, you will have a position of authority in your life.
- If you dream of someone taking a crown off of your head, you will lose your position of authority.
- If you dream of giving someone a crown, you are going to give them an important position in your life.
- If you dream of taking a crown from off your own head and giving it to someone, you will pass your authority on to that person.

D

dancing

- If you dream of dancing alone, it is a sign of joy to come.
- If you dream of dancing with someone, take note of who the person is and if your movements together are harmonious or awkward. If they

are harmonious, you may become "partnered" successfully with this person in business or in love. If your movements are awkward, you should stay away from them.

dead

- If you dream of a dead person and they speak directly to you, pay very close attention to their message. There is something significant in that message for you.
- If you dream of a departed loved one in the company of others, take note of who the other people are. If any of them are alive currently, they will soon pass away.

death

- If you dream of someone who is already dead, there will be rain.
- If you dream of seeing a dead person and they are smiling at you, all will be well.
- If you dream of seeing a dead person and they are crying, sorrow is not long off.
- If you dream of seeing a dead person and they are telling you something, listen carefully. They are bringing you important news.
- To dream of death is a sign that there will be a birth.

devil

- If you dream of the devil, rebuke him in the name of Jesus.
- If you dream of the devil stealing your soul, that is a warning that he is trying to lead you down the wrong path.

Murray Hill

diamonds

- If you dream of owning diamonds, you will have wealth.
- If you dream of receiving diamonds, you will have love.
- If you dream of wearing diamonds, you will have power.
- If you dream of losing diamonds, you will have sorrow.

dogs

- To dream of a dog as a companion shows that you have faithful friends.
- To dream of a fat dog means prosperity.
- To dream of a skinny dog means hard times ahead.
- To dream of a barking dog means that you will hear depressing news.
- To dream of a dead dog means that evil is afoot. Be careful.
- If you sleep on a dog's pillow, you will dream the dog's dreams. If your dog knows something you need to know, he will show you in the dream.

dragonfly (also known as snake doctor or snake feeder)

- If you dream of a dragonfly, it means the same as dreaming of a butterfly. (see butterfly)
- If a dragonfly lands on you in a dream, you will have good luck.
- If a dragonfly perches on your hand in a dream, it is trying to speak to you with a specific message and you need to pay close attention to what happens next in the dream.
- If a dragonfly lands on something in your dream and you can't shoo it away, you have unexpected company coming.

dream

- If you want to have sweet dreams, put a pinch of sugar under your pillow at night.
- Sleep with a mirror under your pillow and you will see your true love when you dream.
- If you want to dream of who you will marry, this is what you do. Boil an egg hard. Take the yellow out of the middle and fill it up with salt. Do NOT drink anything after you eat it and before you go to sleep. If you dream of someone bringing you a drink of water, whoever brings it is the person you are going to marry.
- If you don't want to have bad dreams, don't eat late at night.
- If you dream that you are dreaming, you have power within the dream to use your own will to change the outcome and ending of the dream. Pay close attention to the message.

driving

- If you dream of driving over a smooth road that is clearly marked, the answer to whatever decisions you are about to make will be clear and the outcome will be good.
- If you dream of driving over rough, rocky, excessively curvy, or rugged road, you have difficulties in your life and you must be careful about the decisions you make.
- If someone else is driving you to a destination, you have a time of rest and peace coming.

E

enemy

- If you dream of someone chasing you, you have an enemy.
- If you dream of hiding from a person, that person is your enemy.
- If you dream that someone is chasing you, but you escape, you know that you have an enemy, but everything will turn out right for you in the end.

F

falling

- If you dream of falling off a cliff and don't wake up, you will die.
- If you dream of falling and you catch yourself and wake up, bad luck is on the way.

fingers

- If you cross your fingers before you go to sleep and sleep with them crossed, you will not have bad dreams.

fire

- If you dream of fire, you will be angry.
- If you dream of a consuming fire, loss is at hand.
- If you dream of a fire that does not consume, trouble may come, but it will not destroy you.

fish

- If you dream of a fish, someone you know is going to have a baby.
- If you dream of swallowing a fish, you are going to have a baby.
- If you dream of a goldfish, someone will soon be in love with you.
- If you dream of a fish, it is a sign that there will be a new addition to the family—a baby, or a marriage.

flying

- To dream of flying is a sign of you moving upward in your life or career.

fruit

- If you dream of perfect fruit, it is a sign of prosperity coming to you.
- If you dream of wormy fruit it is a sign of disappointment coming to you.
- If you dream of bruised fruit it signifies something is going wrong in your life that you are not yet aware of.
- If you dream of withered fruit, it is a sign of difficulties or loss coming to you.
- If you dream of a fruitless tree in bearing season in a specific person's yard, beware of that person. They are false. Their words and their life will bear no fruit.

funeral

- If you dream of a funeral, someone close to you will get very sick or someone is going to die.

G

garden

- To dream of working in a garden means that you have things in your life that must be attended too quickly.
- If you dream of a full, lush garden, you have prosperity coming into your life.

Bud and Benny Fultz
Twila, KY

- If you dream of a withered, unproductive garden, there will be hard times ahead.
- If you dream of a weedy garden, there are things in your life that you need to remove.

garlic

- Put a string of garlic on your bed post to keep away bad dreams.

ghost

- Wear a pouch of salt around your neck to keep ghosts away and out of your dreams.
- Draw a circle around your bed to keep ghosts away from your sleep.

gloves

- If you dream of finding a pair of matched gloves, a good opportunity is coming your way.
- If you dream of holding one glove in your hand and finding the match to it, love is coming into your life.
- If you dream of holding one glove in your hand and hunting for the other glove that is lost, you will lose a love from your life.

gold

- If you dream of finding a piece of gold, or any object made of gold, you are going to come into some money.
- If you dream of losing anything made of gold, you are going to lose money.

H

hair

- If you dream of getting your hair cut, you will be ashamed of something in the near future.
- If you dream that you have long, flowing hair, you will be blessed.
- If you dream of trying to comb tangles out of your hair, you have confusion in your life.

honey

- If you dream of eating honey, you are loved.
- If you dream of someone eating honey at your table, they love you.
- If you dream of someone holding a jar of honey, they have something you want.
- If you dream of giving honey to someone, you will give your love to them.

horse

- If you dream of a white horse, someone will die.
- If you dream of riding a horse easily, all will be well.
- If you dream of riding a horse and having trouble staying seated or falling off, trouble is coming your way.

house

- If you dream of moving into a beautiful house, your life is going to improve.
- If you dream that you are lost in a house and can't find your way out, someone is trying to find you.
- If you dream of wandering through a strange house, you are unsettled in your life and searching for answers.
- If you dream of hiding in a house, you have fears that you haven't faced.
- If you dream of finding new rooms in a house, rooms you didn't know were there, something good is coming to your life.
- The dream you have the first night you sleep in a new house will surely come true.

I

ink

- If you dream of spilling ink that you can't clean up, you are going to be involved in a scandal.
- If you dream of ink stains on your clothes or skin, something you've done in secret will be exposed.

- If you dream of successfully cleaning up ink or ink stains, your troubles will pass.

J

jail
- If you dream of seeing someone you know in jail, be careful of that person. They may be dishonest and deliberately trying to deceive you.
- If you dream that you are in jail, you will be publicly shamed.
- If you dream of a loved one getting out of jail and you are happy about it, they will change their behavior for the good.
- If you dream of wanting someone to go to jail, it signifies your desire to have them out of your life and to be free of them or safe from them.

K

keys
- To dream of keys means change is coming into your life.
- If you dream that you are holding unfamiliar keys, it means you will have an opportunity for change that is good.
- If you dream of someone else holding keys, they may hold the opportunity for your life that is good.
- If you dream of losing keys, that means opportunity has passed you by.

knife
- If you dream of a knife, you are going to experience pain somewhere in your life.

L

letter
- If you dream of receiving a letter from the person you love, it means they love you, too.

- If you dream of getting a letter from someone important in your life who has passed on, it means they had unfinished business with you and the message in the letter is what they would have wanted to say to you.
- If you dream of getting a letter from a distant friend, they will soon pay you a visit.
- If you dream of reading a letter from an unknown source, pay close attention to the details. There is a message there for you.

light

- If you are alone in the dark and cannot find the light switch, it represents fear in your life
- If you are in the dark and see any kind of a light in the distance, it means you will find a way through your troubles. Help will come.
- If you light a candle in the darkness in a dream, you will help someone through a hard time and give them hope.

lost things

- If you dream of something you've lost and it is in a very specific place in the dream, when you wake up go look for your lost object and it will be in that place.

M

magic

- If you dream that you are performing magic in a dream, it means you are looking for solutions to troubles.
- If someone else is performing magic in a dream, it means They are deceitful.

marriage

- If you tape mistletoe on the ceiling above your bed, on Christmas Eve you will dream of the person you are going to marry.

Hershel Young, Jr. and sister Elizabeth Young—Putney, KY

- If you dream of a marriage or a wedding in your family, it is a sign of death in your family.
- If you dream of a marriage between strangers, someone new is coming into your family.
- If you dream of a faceless person, who embraces or kisses you, that is an assurance that you will marry. You just haven't met that person yet.
- If you want to know who you will marry, do the following. Boil an egg hard. Cut it in half and take out the yolk. Fill the space the yolk left with salt and eat the whole thing without drinking any liquid afterward or talking to anyone. Go to bed and go to sleep. You will dream of someone of the opposite sex bringing you a drink of water. If that person is single, that is the person you are going to marry.

money

- To dream of silver money is a lucky dream.
- To dream of paper money means that good luck is coming your way.

morning

- Morning dreams come true.
- If you tell a dream before breakfast, it will come true.

mud/muddy

- If you dream of being covered in mud, it means you have trouble coming to you.
- If you dream of muddy water, it represents troubles in your life and decisions that are unclear.
- If you dream of seeing a particular person standing in muddy water, that person has trouble in their life.
- When dreaming of muddy water, the darker the color of mud, the more serious the warning is and the more danger you are in.

N

nakedness

- If you dream of a naked man, a man in your family will die.

- If you dream of a naked man you do not know, a woman is going to die.
- If you dream of a naked woman, a woman in your family will die.
- If you dream of a naked woman that you do not know, a man is going to die.
- If you dream that you are naked and trying to cover up, it means you are going to be brought to an open shame.

Ollie Couch, Polly Turner, Bill Turner, Carson Neff, Sally and Sid Hyder—Big Laurel, KY

necklace

- If you dream of getting a necklace, it is a sign of blessing.
- If you dream of giving a necklace, it is a sign of love.
- If you dream of losing a necklace, it means losing a love.

needle

- If you dream of sewing with a needle, mending fabric, it means that your troubles will be mended.
- In a dream, sewing with a needle to repair someone else's garments means they have illness coming and will have need of your help.
- If you dream of searching for a needle you've lost, trouble is coming.
- If you dream of trying to thread the eye of a needle and are successful, your current project will work out well.
- If you dream of trying to thread the eye of a needle but with many attempts cannot do it, you will not be successful in your current project. Let it go.

New Year's Day

- If you dream of leaving clothes hanging on the line on New Year's Day or you will have bad luck all year long.
- If you dream of doing a particular thing on New Year's Day as the year comes in, you will be doing that thing the rest of the year.

nightmares

- If you put a sprig of holly on the head of your bed, you will not have bad dreams.

John and Dora Taylor Family

- If you sleep with a Bible under your pillow, you will not have bad dreams.
- If you don't eat after 6:00 p.m., you will not have bad dreams.
- If you lay on your back to sleep, you will have bad dreams.
- If you say your prayers before you go to sleep, you will not have nightmares.
- If you put garlic salt in the four corners of your bedroom, you will never have nightmares.
- If you are having nightmares, sprinkle a circle of salt all the way around your bed. The nightmares will end.

nose

- If you dream that your nose itches, someone is coming.

O

ocean

- If you dream of standing on the beach, looking out at the ocean with peaceful waves lapping around you, all will be well with you.
- If you dream of standing on the beach, looking out at a stormy sea, trouble or danger is headed your way.

ogre

- If you dream of an ogre locking you in a dungeon, and you can't get out, you will never wake up.

P

present

- If you dream of receiving a present, you are going to get a good surprise.

Q

queen

- If you dream of a queen in your life, she represents someone in authority, or she may represent someone standing between you and the thing you want to achieve.

quilt

- If you dream while sleeping under a new quilt that no one else has slept under before, your dream is sure to come true.

R

raccoon

- To dream of a raccoon means that someone in your life is trying to steal something from you.

rape

- If you dream of being violated physically, you are in harm's way — emotionally or physically, or perhaps both.
- If you dream of a specific person raping you, stay away from them completely. Cut them out of your life.

repeated dreams

- If you dream the same dream three times, that dream will come true.
- If you dream a dream many times, there is a message for you in the dream that you need to figure out which will help you in your life. Once you discover the message of the dream, you won't ever dream it again.
- If two people dream the same dream on the same night, it will come true.

rose

- If you dream of receiving a rose that smells good from a member of the opposite sex, that person is interested in you.
- If you dream of receiving a rose from a member of the opposite sex and you are pricked by a thorn on that rose, this person will bring sorrow into your life.

- If you dream of being given a rose and putting it in your hair, someone whom you trust is deceiving you.
- To dream of being given a bouquet of roses is a sign of joy coming.
- To dream of a rose bush in full bloom means great joy coming your way.
- Dreaming of dead roses represents sadness.

S

Saturday

- Saturday dreamed and Sunday told
  Is sure to come true, before a month old.

season

- Dream something out of season, it means trouble out of reason.

shoes

- If you dream of shoes that fit too tight, your walk through life is going to be a hard one.
- If you don't want to dream, put your shoes under the foot of your be before you go to sleep at night.
- If you dream of comfortable shoes, your walk through life will be a comfortable one.
- If you dream you've lost your shoes, you may have lost your way in life.
- If you dream of searching for your shoes, you are searching for answers in your life and want to make the right choices.

*Smith and Eager Logging Team
1903 — Harlan, KY*

sleepwalking

- If you wake someone up who is sleep walking, they will go into shock.

snake

- If you dream of a snake, you have an enemy.
- If you dream of being bitten by a snake, your enemy will hurt you in some way.

Calvin Hensley Grist Mill
Martin's Fork, KY

- If you dream of a snake trying to bite you, but not able to break the skin, your enemy will make an attempt to harm you, but that attempt will fail.
- If you dream of killing a snake, you will overcome your enemy.
- If you dream of a snake running away from you, be careful. Your enemy has gone into hiding. You may not be able to recognize the person who intends to harm you.
- If you dream of cutting a snake's head off, you will stop the rumors that are being spread about you.
- If you dream of a person with a snake's tongue, that person speaks evil of you and is dangerous or a rumormonger.
- If you dream of a snake talking, someone is lying to you.
- If you dream of snakes surrounding you, it means troubles and trials surround you.
- If you dream of seeing someone talking and a snake's tongue shoots out of their mouth, they are talking bad about you or lying to you.

snow
- To dream of snow is a sign of disappointment to come.
- To dream of snow signifies a loss of something or someone.

spiders
- To dream of a spider is good luck, unless you kill it.
- If you dream of killing a spider, you have an enemy.

sweet
- If you want to have sweet dreams, put a pinch of sugar beneath your pillow before you go to sleep at night.

T

Elvita Smile and Son

teeth

- If you dream of losing a tooth, a family member will die.
- If you dream of your teeth falling out, someone in your family is going to be very ill, but if you dream that the tooth grows back, they will recover from their illness.
- If you dream of your teeth falling out, someone in your family is going to die *or* you are going to lose a friend of great importance to you. *But* if you dream of the tooth growing back, that person will be replaced by someone special who comes into your life.
- If you dream of losing a tooth, you will lose a friend.
- If you dream of your teeth crumbling, you will lose someone you love.
- If in your dream you have a mouth full of rotten or crooked teeth, you are guilty of saying things that have hurt others.
- If you dream of someone with rotten teeth, they are a liar.

telling

- Don't tell your dream before breakfast if you want it to come true.
- If you had a bad dream, you have to remember it and tell it before breakfast to keep it from coming true.
- If someone tells you they love you in a dream, you cannot repeat it to another soul until they actually say it to you in real life, if you want it to come true.
- If you dream of something you really, really want to come true, you mustn't ever tell anyone.

W

wake

- If you are in the middle of a bad dream and you know that you are dreaming, tell yourself to wake up and you will.

water (see also **mud/muddy**)

- If you dream of clear water that you can see through like glass, it is a sign of good things ahead.
- If you dream of black water, it is a sign of impending death.
- Stormy water, or churning water means there are troubled days ahead.
- Moving water (like a river or an ocean) that carries you away symbolizes a direction that you are headed and you need to ride out the situation, knowing that you will arrive safely at your destination.
- Obstacles in the water represent obstacles in your life.

wedding

- If you dream of a wedding and see a person dressed in white, that person is going to die.
- If you are single and dream of a faceless person, it means you have not met your bride or groom yet.

William A. Randall, Bradley Gross,
and Henry Bennett—Twila, KY
1952

Fowler family

≈ Home Remedies ≈

Mossie and Ramona Saylor

Home remedies that were once used (or some that perhaps still are) often sound worse than the original condition. The following information is recorded not as accurate medical cures, but rather for the purely interesting aspect of the content. It is not recommended that anyone try any of these.

A

abscess

- Make yellow oak ooze and hold it on a sore gum to draw the poison out of an abscess.

acne

- Take a garlic capsule daily to help cure acne.
- Rub fresh garlic on acne sores.
- Tea tree oil on pimples will help acne go away.
- Mix flour, honey, and vinegar into a paste and put it on acne.
- Coat your acne with toothpaste before you go to sleep at night.
- Wash your face with a wet diaper.
- Dip a washcloth in a mixture of urine and water. Ring it out and wash your face with it from time to time to help avoid acne.
- Rub strawberries on your face to cure acne.
- Rub a slice of apple on acne to make it go away.

aging

- Eating blueberries will slow down the effects of aging.
- To slow aging, find something to do outside at least half an hour each day.

allergies

- Take one teaspoon of wild honey every day that was gathered from hives where you live.
- Take evening primrose to help relieve allergies.
- Take virgin olive oil and put a little up your nose. It keeps pollen and dust from getting in our sinuses, down our throat, in your lungs, and keeps them from sticking to the inside of your nose.
- Ground hog grease inside the nose will accomplish the same as the olive oil mentioned above.

Alzheimer

- Daffodil tea will help fight Alzheimer's.

anemia

- Eat lots of fresh vegetables.
- Make sure red meat is on your diet every day.
- Eat the yolks from duck eggs to cure anemia.
- Eat lots of liver.
- Eat raw liver.

antiseptic

- Boil some goldenseal root to use an antiseptic and as an astringent.
- Boil some ginseng to make an antiseptic wash for sores. Also, taking ginseng tablets or drinking ginseng tea helps cleanse the body of bacteria.
- Boil camphor vine to make an antiseptic wash.

apples

- An apple a day keeps the doctor away.
- Eat an apple every day with the peel on to help with constipation.

arthritis

- Drink tea made from the seeds of alfalfa.
- Boil pokeberries and put the liquid on sore joints.
- Boil pokeberries and drink the juice.
- Rub skunk oil on arthritic joints.
- Rub liquor on the sore joint regularly.
- Massage the sore joint daily with warm oil.
- Use cohosh root to make a tea and drink it every day to help relieve pain of arthritis.
- Eat lots of celery to help with arthritis or rheumatism and gout.
- Massage the aching area to ease the arthritis pain.
- Take a hot soapy bath. While you are in the tub, wrap a towel around the sore joint and keep it there until you are ready to get out of the bath.
- Wear a gold ring and it will help lessen arthritis pain.
- To relieve arthritis, carry a raw potato in your pocket.

Geraldine Hensley   *Letha Hensley*

- Hold a magnet on a sore joint to draw out the pain.
- A teaspoon of honey a day will help fight arthritis pain.
- Soak sore joints in Epsom salts and hot water.
- Eat two or three pokeberries a day for arthritis pain. They can be dried and saved over the winter and taken two or three times a day.
- Place fresh chicken droppings under the bed each night.
- Wear loafers with a new penny in each shoe.
- Take a dead cat, rub it on the arthritis areas and bury the cat in a hollow stump in the woods.
- Ginseng tea is good to take for arthritis.
- Mix turpentine with an egg yolk and rub it on the arthritic joint(s) daily.
- Mix a pinch of gunpowder into a glass of whole milk. Drink this mixture every day until the pain lets up.
- Carry a horse chestnut in your pocket to keep arthritis away.
- Nuss a cat in your lap to help relieve arthritis.
- Drink coconut milk from the shell and eat the flesh of fresh coconut on an empty stomach to help relieve arthritis pain.
- Drink sassafras tea daily to ease arthritis pain.
- Rub ginseng root on an arthritic joint to relieve the pain.
- Rub earthworm grease on an arthritic joint to ease the pain.
- Grind up goldenseal root and put it in whiskey. Take a spoon full every now and then.
- A bee sting on an arthritic joint will help ease the arthritis.

asthma (sometimes referred to as **tiz**)

- Swallow a handful of spider web balls.
- Buy a Chihuahua and keep it in your house and your asthma will disappear.
- If a child has asthma, take them to a tree in the woods and drive a nail in the tree an inch or two taller than the child. When the child grows past the nail, the asthma will be gone.
- Smoke jimson weed to cure asthma.
- Tansy tea is good to relieve asthma.
- If a child has asthma, cut a sourwood switch slightly longer than the child is tall and put it between the child's mattresses. When they outgrow the length of the switch, their asthma will go away.
- Take a teaspoon of honey from your own bees every day and it will keep you from having asthma.
- Put salt in a brown paper bag and breathe in and out of the bag when your asthma is acting up.
- Chew on honeycomb fresh from the hive to clear up an asthma attack.
- If you have bees, get pollen from the honey traps and take a little of the pollen every day. It will relieve your asthma.
- Drink hot coffee to help soothe asthma attacks.
- Cut a sourwood stick two inches taller than the growing child who has asthma and hide it above the door post the child comes in and out of. When the child grows taller than the switch, their asthma will be gone.
- Cut a sourwood stick and measure it by the baby or child who has asthma. Take the sourwood stick to a swampy place and throw it down. Don't look back and walk away. When the child outgrows the size of the stick, the asthma will go away.

William Creech and Sally Dixon Pine Mountain, KY

- Drink hot tea with honey and lemon to ease an asthma attack.

- Boil eucalyptus and breathe the vapors.

athlete's foot

- Soak your feet in a mixture of two teaspoons of salt per pint of warm water.
- Take one (1) cup of marigold petals and ½ cup of petroleum jelly (4 ounces). Mix them together in a pan and fry them on low heat for 30 minutes. Strain through a cheese cloth to clear. Store in a jar. Rub nightly as needed on feet. Make sure to wear socks to bed in order to keep the ointment off the covers!
- Urinate on your feet nightly until the athlete's foot disappears.
- Soak your feet in ice water nightly to cure athlete's foot.
- Wash your feet with a damp dishrag dipped in Clorox. It will cure athlete's foot.

B

baby

- To help soothe a fussy baby, put butter and honey in a small bag for the baby to suck on.

back ache

- Soak in a hot tub of water to ease a back ache.
- Drink cranberry juice to help cleanse kidneys, which may in turn relieve a back ache.

Wash Fee; unidentified

- Eat lots of fiber in your diet to avoid constipation, which may in turn relieve a back ache.
- If you sleep on your side, put a pillow between your knees at night.
- If you sleep on your back, put a pillow under your knees at night.

bad breath

- Chew some fresh parsley after every meal. This works!

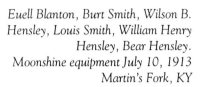

*Euell Blanton, Burt Smith, Wilson B.
Hensley, Louis Smith, William Henry
Hensley, Bear Hensley.
Moonshine equipment July 10, 1913
Martin's Fork, KY*

- Put two drops of tea tree oil on your toothbrush along with toothpaste to freshen your breath longer.
- If you've eaten garlic, drink pineapple juice afterwards. It will clear out the garlic smell.
- For bad breath, chew some cloves of fennel.
- Drink a hot cup of coffee to clear up an asthma attack.
- Suck on a lemon wedge after eating garlic or onion to improve bad breath.
- Eating tomatoes after a meal with a lot of garlic or onions can improve bad breath.

baldness
- Rub cow manure on the head daily to encourage new hair growth.
- Don't wear baseball caps all the time. Your hair follicles will get too hot and stop growing hair.

bed wetting
- Wash the child's face with the wet sheets from their bed every morning until they quit wetting the bed.
- Suck on cinnamon candy right before bed time.

bee sting (See also **bug bites; stings**)

- Chew up some tobacco and place the cud directly on the bee sting until the fire goes out of the sting.
- To draw a bee's stinger out, lay a copper penny over the sting and it will draw out the stinger.
- Never try to pinch a stinger out of a sting. That can spread more poison. Instead, scrape the stinger out with a flat edged object.
- Soak tobacco in warm water until the water is brown, then paint the bee sting with the tobacco juice until the swelling goes down.
- Make sure the stinger is out of the sting and put beer on the sting.
- Mix honey with a pinch of dirt dauber's nest to make a paste and put it on a bee sting to make it go away.
- Put a bandage over the bee sting and soak it with a strong solution of Epsom salts. Leave it there until it dries completely. When you take it off, it will have drawn the poison out.
- Hold a bee sting over cigarette smoke and it will draw out the poison.
- Soak a bee sting in turpentine.
- Soak a brown paper bag in vinegar and wrap it around the bee sting to draw out the poison.
- Put wet snuff on a bee sting to take the poison out.
- Squirt lemon juice on a bee sting.
- Take a cigarette and break it in two. Soak the tobacco in water and make a poultice to go on the sting.
- Pack the bee sting in mud to draw the poison out.
- Take the ear wax out of your ear and rub it on the bee sting.
- Put mustard on a bee sting to take the swelling out.
- Make a paste of cream of tartar and put it on a bee sting to take the pain and swelling out.
- Put meat tenderizer on the bee sting to take away the pain and make the swelling go down more quickly.
- Slice a fresh onion and put a piece of it over a burn to draw the fire out and to draw the stinger out.

- Rub poke leaves on a sting to take the sting out.
- Boil peach tree leaves for 30–40 minutes. Drain water off of the leaves. Put 1 teaspoon of salt in and thicken with cornmeal to make a poultice. Put it on the area (also works for sores or nail punctures or small wounds) and leave it overnight. This will take out the fever and swelling.
- Moisten baking soda to a paste form with water. Spread it over the bee sting and any swollen area of the skin.
- Make a paste of garlic powder and water. Pack it onto and around the bee sting.
- Put a bandage over the bee sting and soak it with a strong solution of salts.
- Soak the bee sting in hot water, salt, and baking soda.
- Hold something soaked in alcohol over a bee sting until the stinging stops.
- Coal oil on a sting will take the pain away.
- Put poke root juice on a bee sting.
- Put mud on a bee sting.
- Put fresh cow manure on a bee sting.
- Put tree sap on a bee sting.
- Put onion juice on a bee sting.

William and Marie Fowler

*Hensley Brothers
North Carolina?*

*(unknown) Hensley
East Bernstadt, KY*

Emily Creech, Mark and
Susan Turner, Sally Hyder,
unknown, Polly Harris
Big Laurel, KY

- Rub three different kinds of weeds (any kind) on a bee sting to make it go away.

black eye

- Hold a fresh steak on a black eye to take out the bruising.
- Hold a rag soaked in vinegar over a black eye to draw out the color.
- Put toothpaste on the discolored tissue around the eye (but not on the eyelid) to draw out the bruise.

bleeding

- Place a green leaf over a wound and wrap it up on top of the wound. This will help stop the bleeding.
- Gather fresh spider webs in the morning dew and ball them up. Let them dry in the sun, and then store them in a jar. If you get an open wound, press some of the spider web into the wound and it will help clot the blood.
- Hold a brown paper bag tightly over the wound.
- Pack the wound with dirt.
- Pack the wound with moss.
- Hold a flat piece of glass over the wound and press.
- Take soot black from the chimney or fireplace and daub it on the wound to stop blood flow from a wound.

- Dried leaves pressed in to a wound will make it stop bleeding.
- Put soot from the stove or fireplace on a cut to stop the bleeding.
- Pack the wound with a paste of white sugar and turpentine.
- Apply a poultice of brown sugar soaked in turpentine to the wound to stop bleeding.
- Quote the Bible verse Ezekiel 16:6: "And when I passed by thee and saw thee polluted in thine own blood, I said unto thee, when thou was in the blood, Live; yea, I said unto then when thou wast in thy blood LIVE!"

blister

- If you get a blister, don't burst it until after the sun goes down.
- If you get a blister, let it pop on its own. Cover it and keep it clean.

blood — To purify

- Eat ramps as a spring blood tonic to purify the blood.
- Poke sallet is a good spring tonic to purify the blood and body of toxins collected over the winter.
- Eat lots of greens to help keep your blood system cleaned out.
- Drink sassafras tea to keep the blood purified.
- Drink red sassafras root tea to purify the blood.
- Eat garlic and/or onions as a regular part of your diet to help purify the blood.

blood poisoning

- Pack the infected area with cow dung to draw the poison out.

blood pressure

- Squeeze your fists as tight as you can and then relax them. Do this several times until you feel your blood pressure going back down.
- Eat lots of garlic or take garlic tablets to help control high blood pressure.
- Eat gen sang to help lower blood pressure.

Alma Jean and Polly Couch — Putney, KY

- Drink sassafras tea to help control high blood pressure.
- Cumin acts as a blood thinner.

bloody nose

- Wear a Yankee dime around the neck to prevent nose bleeds.
- Chew paper to stop a nosebleed.
- Fold a piece of brown paper bag and put it between gums and lips to stop a nosebleed.

body odors

- Mix vanilla extract, water, and rubbing alcohol. Shake well. Put it on your body after you shower for a nice clean scent.
- Put Milk of Magnesia on a cotton ball and use it under your arms instead of deodorant after you shower.
- Chunky peanut butter applied to the underarms and rubbed off will take away underarm smell.
- Take two zinc tablets, 50 mg per tablet twice a day for a week. It will stop body odors.
- Soak cotton pads in vanilla. Rub them on the area that smells bad.
- Drink 12 oz. of tomato juice a day for a week. Then drink the same amount 2–3 times per week. Once the body odor has cleared up, drink the tomato juice as needed.

boil

- Place raw potato slices on a boil, cover with a bandage and it will help to draw the boil to a head.
- Heat a glass pop bottle in hot water until the bottle is hot (but not hot enough to burn the skin). Dry the bottle around the rim. Turn it upside down over the boil and hold it securely in place until it cools. It will draw the head of the boil to the top of the skin.
- Scorch a plantain leaf and cover a boil with it. Wrap it in place overnight. It will draw the boil to a head.
- Beat the roots of a slippery elm tree into a poultice. Pack it onto the boil. Wrap. It will draw the boil to a head.

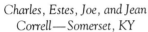

Charles, Estes, Joe, and Jean Correll—Somerset, KY   *Ollie and Zola Couch*

- Spread the pulp of figs, prunes, or raisins on a boil and cover with a bandage to draw the poison to the surface.
- Take the inside lining of the egg shell and place over a boil. Cover with a bandage and leave for three days. It will draw the poison out of the boil.
- A boil will not go away until you draw the core to the top of the skin (a head) and get it out.
- Put sweet potato pulp on a boil and cover it to draw the boil to a head. It may take a few days. Change the sweet potato pulp and bandage daily.
- Mix soap powder into a paste and add sugar. Cover the boil with this mixture to draw the boil out.
- Heat slices of an onion in the microwave. Lay the heated (not too hot) slices over the boil. Bandage it and leave it overnight or all day. It will draw the boil out.
- After the core has come out of a boil, pack salt in the opening to help draw out the poison.
- Put lard or salt pork on top of a boil and bandage it that way overnight to draw it to a head.
- Scrape an Irish potato into a pulp. Put a small handful over the boil and bandage it securely in place overnight. It will draw the poison out of the boil. If one time doesn't do the job, repeat.

broken bones

- If you think you've broken a bone and it feels like fire running out of the spot, it is most likely broken.

- If you get hit in the nose and your eyes turn black, your nose is probably broken.
- If you break a bone, water will come to the top and make a swollen knot of skin over the break.

bruises

- Make a poultice of wild indigo to draw the color out of a bruise.
- Make a toothpaste poultice to draw out a bruise.
- Soak the bruise in vinegar daily and it will vanish more quickly.
- Soak a bruise in vinegar to take away the pain.
- Soak a brown paper bag in vinegar and wrap it around the bruise to take away the swelling and the coloring.
- Lay raw meat on a bruise to take out swelling, soreness, and coloring.
- Make a poultice of little bits of a brown paper bag soaked in vinegar. Place the poultice over a bruise and wrap it with a bandage. When the poultice is completely dried out, it will lift right off of the area. Repeat until the bruising is gone.

bug bites

- Moisten your skin over the bite and rub an aspirin over the area.
- Rub fresh parsley over a bug bite to take out the itch.
- Put a drop of ammonia on a bug bite or sting to draw out the poison and help the bite to heal more quickly.
- Put raw onions on a bug bite to draw out the itch.

Leona Turner Couch, Alice Lyons

- Place a slice of raw potato over a bug bite to take out the itch and help it go away.
- Apple cider vinegar on a bug bite will make it heal faster.
- Toothpaste on a bug bite will provide relief from the itch.
- Meat tenderizer on a bug bite will draw out the itch.
- A salt poultice on a bug bite will help dry it up.

- Raw honey on a bug bite will do the trick to take out the itch.
- Lemon juice will neutralize the itch of a bug bite.
- Green herbs rubbed on a bug bite will help relieve the itch such as comfrey, plantain, savory, or just ordinary grass. The herbs release chlorophyll which eases the pain. Rub any of these vigorously on bites and stings to relieve the itch, the pain, and help them heal faster.

Ollie Turner
Berea, KY

burns

- Put mustard on a burn to help take out the sting.
- Put fresh calf dung on a burn.
- Mustard on a burn will help it to heal without a scar.
- Rub a live forever flower on a burn.
- Split a vitamin E oil capsule in half and put the oil on a burn to help it heal faster.
- Hold the burn in ice water until the stinging stops. This will draw the fire out.
- Put raw potato peelings on a burn.
- Put vinegar on a burn.
- Grate fresh Arsh (Irish; white) potatoes and put on a mild burn. When the potatoes get warm, put fresh ones on. They draw out the burn and keep it cool. The cool potatoes will help the pain, also.
- Dip a piece of brown paper bag in vinegar and hold it over a burn until it stops hurting.
- Dip a piece of brown paper bag in vinegar and place it on the burn, then wrap the burn with the piece of paper bag over the burn to help it heal faster.
- Rub unsalted butter on a burn to ease the pain.
- For a minor burn, soak it in milk.
- Paint a burn with toothpaste to take the fire out.

Sally Clark Eager,
DOB 1860—Wythe
County, VA

Joni Muncy

- The juice from an aloe plant will heal a first degree burn.
- Hold a burn in cold water to draw out the pain.
- Cut an Irish potato in thin slices and place them on the burn.
- If you burn yourself, hold the burn next to a source of heat or a hot surface and it will draw the heat out of the burn.
- Put snuff on a burn. Cover it with a cold rag. It will take the pain away.
- Put mayonnaise on a fresh burn until it melts.
- Put old timey liniment on a burn to draw out the pain.
- Put evaporated milk on a burn to take the pain away and cause it to heal faster.
- Soak a burn in peroxide.
- Take table salt and dissolve it in warm water, soak a bandage in the water, then wrap it around a burn. It will keep it from getting infected and it will heal faster.
- Catch the first snow of winter and let it melt in a mason jar. If you get burned any time that year, put the snow water on the burn and it will take the pain away. Make sure to empty out the old water and catch the first snow of the next season to have on hand, if needed.
- Take the soot off of the cool eye of a wood burning stove to cure a burn.
- Melt tallow and smooth it over a burn. Wrap it in a clean dry cloth.
- Make fresh mint tea. Let it cool. Pour it over the burn or soak the burn in it until the fire stops burning in the wound.

C

camphor

DO NOT DRINK THIS MIXTURE! It is to rub on or smell ONLY.

To make homemade camphor you will need ½ pint of pure corn moonshine or ½ pint of grain alcohol. You will also need 2 blocks of Gum Camphor. Break up the blocks of camphor in very small pieces. It can be broken up by wrapping it in 2 layers of cloth and hitting it with a hammer until it is in very small pieces. DO NOT USE RUBBING ALCOHOL! Mix in the grain alcohol or moonshine with the pieces of camphor. Keep the mixture covered tight. It is good to smell this mixture for a mild sick stomach. You can also smell of it to cure a mild headache. Also, it is good to rub gently on gnat bites, mosquito bites, and mild bruises. It is very good for cold sores, but it will sting.

cancer

- Eating fresh May apples will help fight cancer.
- Dry May apples and eat one daily to help fight cancer.
- Eat lots of blueberries when you are young and you won't have cancer when you grow up.
- Bloodroot will help shrink tumors.
- Use cumin to fight cancer.

chaffing

- Sprinkle baby powder generously on the chaffed area.
- Sprinkle corn starch generously on the chaffed area.
- Remove clothing from the chaffed area at night and let the air get to it.

chapped lips

- Rub ear wax on chapped lips to heal them.
- Use castor oil on chapped lips.
- Use vitamin E oil on chapped lips.
- Olive oil is good to use on chapped lips.
- Put cooking grease on chapped lips.

Sterling and Jeanette McDaniels

- The juice from an aloe plant will help chapped lips.
- Lemon juice on chapped lips will help them heal quicker.

chapped hands

- Wash or pick wool. The lanolin in the wool is good for your hands.
- Cover your hands in Vaseline and put on a pair of cotton gloves. Sleep in the gloves. Do this every night until the hands are cured.
- Use olive oil on chapped hands. Rub in gently until the oil is absorbed and not greasy on the skin.

chicken

- If you don't want a chicken's eggs to hatch, grease them with Vaseline.

chicken pox

- Take a bath in oatmeal to ease the itch of chicken pox and make the sores dry up.
- Drink catnip tea to reduce fever from chicken pox.
- Boil oatmeal in a lot of water. When the mixture cools, use the oatmeal water to paint on chicken pox. It will relieve the itch.

chiggers (some call jiggers)

- Put clear finger nail polish over a chigger bite to smother it out.
- Put Vaseline over a chigger bite to smother it out.
- Put salt and grease on a chigger bite to kill it out.
- Put some Clorox in your bathwater to kill chiggers.

Roxie, Buddy and Buster Rowland, Jennifer and Theresa McDaniels

- Paint chigger bites with a mixture of salt and grease.
- Rub Clorox on chigger bites.
- Burn a sewing needle. Stick the needle in salty water and then poke the bite. It will make it go away
- Put tobacco juice on chigger bites to get rid of the itch and the swelling.

- Anything thick like a salve, lotion, or ointment, which will cover a chigger bite and smother the chigger, will work to relieve chigger bites.

clogged arteries (see also blood)

- Drink lots of grape juice to avoid clogged arteries.

cold

- Make yellow oak ooze from the bark. Swallow some to cure a cold.
- To help avoid getting a cold in the first place, eat onion sandwiches.
- For a head cold take sassafras root.
- Mix castor oil in orange juice, lemon juice, or sweet tea and drink it. Make tea from the leaves of boneset. Drink the tea cool. It will make you sick if you drink it hot. You can dry the leaves and save them to use in winter.
- Wear garlic around your neck to keep a cold away.
- For a chest cold, make a chest poultice from camphorated oil poured on warm rags or towels and placed directly on the person's chest.
- Mix camphor and goose grease to put on a person's chest that has lung congestion.
- Make a poultice of goose grease and place it directly on the person's chest.
- Take a dose of charcoal powder mixed with honey to cure a cold.
- Fry onions and make a poultice to put on your chest to control a cold and keep away lung fever (pneumonia).
- When you first think you may be coming down with a cold, sniff a little salt water up your nose and gargle some salt water. It may stop the cold before it takes hold.
- To cure a cold, swallow a teacup of vinegar and honey mixed in equal amounts.
- Chew horsemint to relieve a cold.
- Chew the leaves and stems of a peppermint plant to get rid of a cold.
- Cook onions and place them between two layers of towels. Place the warm towels on the person's chest and repeat the process several times as the onions cool.

- Paint the person's chest with mustard and cover it with a towel.
- Take a teaspoon of honey and a glass of milk every day to help avoid colds.
- Drink pepper in whiskey to cure a cold.
- Eat food with lots of garlic or chew garlic clove to help get rid of a cold.
- Use penny royal tea made from the leaves or the roots, served hot, to break a cold.
- For a cold with congestion, put eucalyptus oil in two cups of boiling water and breathe in the steam. This will help relieve the congestion.
- Eat cinnamon candy or cinnamon in other foods to help relieve a cold.
- Mix onion juice, turpentine, and Vicks salve together and put them in a pouch. Wear it around your neck to relieve cold and flu symptoms.
- Mix alcohol, cinnamon candy until it is dissolved, and black pepper together in equal parts. Take it by the teaspoon full to cure a cough or a cold.
- Eat cooked onions to open a stuffy nose.
- When you are eating anything, pour the pepper on while you have a cold.
- Suck on rock candy dipped in moonshine to ease a cold.
- Cut three slices of fresh ginger and bring them to a boil in water. Add two tablespoons of honey and leave to cool. Drink. This remedy works best while a little hot or warm. It will cure a cold.
- Mix one ounce of whiskey with one ounce of lemon juice and one tablespoon of honey. Drink the whole thing down for one dose. Take two or three doses as needed until the cold lets go.
- Make a chest poultice from camphorated oil poured on warm rags or towels and place on the chest. Cover with a warm shirt and get under the covers. Sleep with the poultice over night.
- Make a poultice of goose grease and wrap it around the chest.

cold sore

- Put ear wax on a cold sore to help it heal more quickly.

- Hold a wet tea bag on a cold sore to help it go away.
- Put a drop of any high alcohol content perfume on a cold sore.
- Put yellow root on any kind of mouth sore.

colic

- To cure a baby's colic, give it catnip tea.
- Make a small bag of butter and honey for a baby with colic to suck on.

Hiram and Hannah Lewis

- Let a baby suck on onion juice to cure the colic.
- Put a teaspoon of whisky in the baby's bottle. It will help the baby sleep and control the colic.
- Run a vacuum cleaner to help the baby sleep.
- Take the baby for a ride in a car until it goes to sleep.
- Give the baby honey on its pacifier. It will help the baby sleep.
- Light a pipe, a cigar, or a cigarette in the room with a baby with colic and let it burn on its own. The smoke in the air will help ease colic.
- Mix a tablespoon of honey with water or milk in the baby's bottle to help it sleep.

complexion (see also **Beauty Tips** Section)

- Wash the face with lye soap for a clear complexion.
- Rinse the face with vinegar water to keep a smooth complexion.
- Pat buttermilk over the face and let it dry, then rinse thoroughly before going to bed at night.

constipation

- Eat raw fruit and vegetables to avoid constipation.
- Cook a batch of poke sallet and drain the juice. Drink about half a cup at a time until the constipation is taken care of.
- Drink at least 4 ounces of prune juice daily.
- Use dumago for a laxative.

William Rowland
Putney, KY

- Take two teaspoons of turpentine to get relief from constipation.
- Drink the juice from cooked poke sallet to get bowels moving again.
- Drink ginger tea to help relieve constipation.
- Sit in a tub of cold water.
- Eat a batch of the first greens of spring (any spring green will do).
- Eat green apples.
- Mix a tablespoon of mineral oil as needed to help bowels move more easily.

cough

- Take a teaspoon of honey in your mouth, let it melt slowly and swallow to relieve a cough.
- Chew on raw honeycomb to stop a cough.
- Drink fresh boiled lemon juice to cure a cough.
- Take a little pine tree sap boiled in water with lemon.
- Boil garlic and soak a rag in it. Then wrap the rag around your throat.
- Boil a cow patty in spring water and strain off the water. Use the water to gargle daily. You will have no more cough. This will sooth an itchy throat.
- Bake a large onion (or microwave) and squeeze all the juice out (plus whatever is in the pan). Drink this liquid to cure a cough. You can flavor it with something if necessary or put it in another drink, but it will do the trick.
- Mix wine with equal parts of honey from the comb and lemon juice. Add a tablespoon of ginger. Add one cup of hot water and mix well. Drink the whole glass down.
- Find the wild plant, mullein. Take the leaves off the plant and boil them down in water. Strain that juice through a cloth and put it back on to cook with a cup of honey. Add the juice of two lemons. Mix it all up over the heat until all the honey is dissolved. Boil it down

until it starts getting thick like cough syrup. Take it by the teaspoon whenever you start coughing. It is also good for asthma.

- Make a tea from holly berries. Gargle. Spit out.
- Make a tea from wild cherry bark. Sip it slowly while it is still warm.
- Mash the juice out of an onion. Mix it with honey and take it as needed by the teaspoon full.
- Swallow raw egg whites to ease a cough.
- Mix paregoric with pancake syrup and use it as a cough syrup.
- Slice lemons and boil them with the rind on. Add honey to taste and drink hot.
- Mix one teaspoon of sugar with one teaspoon of whiskey. Heat it over the fire. When the sugar is melted, let it cool a little and take it while it is still warm. It will get rid of a cough.
- Mix lemon juice, rock candy, honey, and whisky or moonshine together in equal measures to make cough syrup.
- Mix honey, soda, and apple cider vinegar together in equal amounts. Take a teaspoon before you go to bed to ease coughing during the night.
- Suck on liquorish.
- Thyme will help ease coughing.
- Boil cherry bark until it makes a tea. Remove the bark. Add sugar. Boil until it thickens to make a cough syrup.
- For a serious cough associated with deep congestion or possible pneumonia, make a hot toddy from equal parts of whisky, honey, lemon, and a tablespoon of ginger. Mix together and heat. Drink a glass full as quickly as possible. Do not sip.
- Mix honey and onions. Cook them together and eat them while they are still warm.
- Take a teaspoon of salt and lick it to get the phlegm out of your throat.
- Bake an onion and when it is done, squeeze the juice out of it and drink it. That will stop a cough.
- Take a teaspoon of straight turpentine. (not recommended since the label notes it as poison)

- Run hot water in the bathroom until the room is very steamy. Sit in the room and breathe the steamy air until the coughing stops.

- Leave an onion in the sun until it is halfway dried out. Then eat little slices of it to cure a cough.

- Cough syrup can be made from honey, lemon, and whisky to be taken a teaspoon at a time as needed.

- Mix ginger, honey, and lemon juice in equal parts. Stir the mixture well and drink it to get rid of a cough.

- If you find a tree in the mountains with a cyst on it, drain the sap from the cyst. Mix it with sugar and water to make a cough syrup.

- A teaspoon of honey and vinegar will cure a cough.

- Rub Vicks Vapor Rub on the bottom of your feet before you go to bed and sleep with socks on.

- Old fashioned cough syrup recipe:
    7 tablespoons of honey
    7 tablespoons of lemon juice
    7 tablespoons of whiskey
Mix the ingredients thoroughly. Take by teaspoons full as needed. Take 1–2 tablespoons of this mixture before going to bed. You can take 1–2 tablespoons every four hours as needed.

- Recipe for cough medicine:
You can use any bottle of any size.
    Fill the bottle half full with moonshine.
    Add ¼ bottle of lemon juice.
    Fill the last ¼ of the bottle with honey.
    Drop in rock candy and yellow root from time to time.
This mixture is good until it is all used up.

croup

- Fried onion juice cures the croup.

- Soak sheep droppings in warm water until they are soft. Rub this over the chest of the person with croup. It will loosen the chest and they can cough up the mucus.

- Wear sheep droppings in a bag around the neck.

crushed finger or toe

- Pour it full of white liniment.

cut

- Paint a cut with tobacco juice to help it heal and take the swelling out.

- Let a dog lick your cut to make it heal faster.

Jerry, Jeanette, William and Roxie Rowland

- Rub blackberries into a cut to help it heal faster and grow back together.

- Pack a cut with axle grease.

- Cover a cut with black tape to help hold it together and keep out germs.

- Pour peroxide in a cut until it boils white. Do this 2–3 times a day until it stops boiling white.

- Fill a cut with white liniment. It will keep it from getting infected. (It also burns like crazy.)

- Coal oil on a cut will help heal it.

- Pack a cut in spider webs to stop bleeding and heal faster.

D

dandruff

- Wash your hair with lye soap.

- Rinse your hair in lime juice.

- Boil pine needles and save the liquid off of them. Mix it with soap.

- suds or shampoo every time you wash your hair. The dandruff will be gone before long.

- Rinse your head in sulfur water after you wash it to cure dandruff. Use one tablespoon of sulfur to one quart of water and this ought to do the trick.

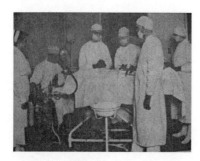

Operating Room—Lynch KY

depression

- Take a teaspoon of honey every day.
- Take a teaspoon of bee pollen every day.

diabetes

- Mix cinnamon and honey (⅛ cup of cinnamon for 1 cup of honey). Take one teaspoon of honey/cinnamon mixture per day.
- Cook with cinnamon as often as possible.
- Avoid all sweet things except fruits.
- Drink lots of water.

diaper rash

- Brown some flour in a skillet on the stove. Let it cool and apply it to a baby's diaper rash.
- Burdock root will help cure diaper rash.
- For diaper rash, rub Crisco onto the area.

diarrhea

- Eat cheese to stop diarrhea.
- Fry flour until it browns and eat it with a spoon.
- Drink dollar leaf tea.
- Boil lady slipper plant in water. Strain the water and drink it.
- Make a tea from red oak bark and drink it.
- Drink rice juice (strained from cooked rice).
- A tablespoon of brown sugar will stop diarrhea.
- Take a dose of castor oil to clean your system of whatever caused the diarrhea in the first place.
- Mix 7-Up and Alka-Seltzer to ease diarrhea.
- Eat a cup of mashed bananas to stop diarrhea.
- Boil plantain in water, strain, and drink a cup full.

- Boil blackberries, strain the water and drink it.
- Take a teaspoon of ground red oak bark.
- Eat cornbread in milk to stop diarrhea.
- Sprinkle black pepper into boiled milk to cure diarrhea.
- Eat peanut butter to stop diarrhea.
- Drink blackberry juice to stop diarrhea.
- Make a tea from sassafras to stop diarrhea.
- Beech bark tea will relieve diarrhea.
- Boiled blackberry root will ease diarrhea.
- Blackberry cordial will check diarrhea.

*George Hensley and
Virgil Hamlin
Martins Fork, KY*

digestion problems

- Suck on cinnamon candy.
- Eat foods with lots of cinnamon.
- Eat fresh poke sallet in the spring as a tonic to clear out the digestive system.
- Take anise for digestive problems.
- Cardamom is an excellent remedy for many digestive problems; helps soothe indigestion, dyspepsia, gastralgia, colon spasms, and flatulence.

diphtheria

- Have the sick person urinate on a cup of carrot greens. Hang the greens in the chimney for a week.

Harlan County Sherriff's Department

55

distemper

- Burn a hornet's nest under a horse's nose to cure distemper.

dizziness

- To cure dizziness, drop a pinch of cayenne pepper into a glass of warm water and sip on it.

diuretic

- Ginseng is a good diuretic.
- Drink cranberry juice or eat whole cranberries as a diuretic.
- One fourth cup of lemon juice will act as a diuretic.
- Eating fresh blueberries will act as a diuretic.

dog remedies

- If your dog gets poisoned, feed it raw eggs.
- If your dog gets worms, put some turpentine in its food.
- If your dog gets the mange, use a mixture of baking soda and lard to put on the infected areas.
- Put brake fluid on the mange.
- Soak a dog with the mange in motor oil.
- Soak a dog with the mange in sulfur and tomato juice.
- Mix sulfur and motor oil together to form a paste.
- Put it on the infected mange area of your dog.

Walter Hamlin and Geneva Hoskins

- If you want a dog to lose pups, feed her blue stone.
- If your dog gets snake bitten, feed it fat meat to draw out the poison.
- Soak a dog with the mange in sulfur and tomato juice.
- Mix sulfur and motor oil together to form a paste. Put it on the infected mange area of your dog.
- If your dog gets snake bitten, feed it fat meat to draw out the poison.

drunk

- Make a drunken person drink black, hot coffee to sober up.
- If a child has drunk liquor by accident, make them drink buttermilk mixed with grease to make them vomit up the liquor.
- Eat milk and bread to absorb excess liquor.

dry skin

- Use virgin olive oil as a moisturizer over the entire body.

Jennifer McDaniels

E

earache

- Lie on your side with the infected ear up; pour warm urine in the ear. Let it sit for a few minutes.
- Put a few drops of warm sassafras tea in the sore ear, let it sit, and then run out after a while.
- Put 2–3 drops of warm baby oil or mineral oil in the ear to relieve an earache.
- Place a hot stone on your ear to draw water out of your ear and relieve an earache.
- Blow tobacco smoke into the sore ear.
- Blow smoke from rabbit tobacco into the sore ear.
- Pour garlic juice in your ear to get rid of an earache.
- Put a drop of garlic oil in the sore ear every night until the earache is gone.
- Put black pepper in a sore ear to cure an earache.
- Chew rabbit fat to relieve an earache.
- Put one drop of cat urine in the sore ear.
- Put a few drops of mother's milk in a sore ear.
- Soak a cotton ball in warm urine. Put it in the sore ear.

Top Row: Robert Smith, Clarence Hamlin, George Hensley, Hamp Hensley Middle Row: Robert Hamlin, George Hamlin, Ead Hamlin, Granville Hamlin Bottom Row: Isaiah Fowler, Quinton Hamlin, Gill Hensley, Sam Hensley

- Put a drop of sweet oil in the ear and seal it with a cotton ball.

- Put the juice of a sow bug in a sore ear.

- Drop a maggot in a severely infected ear. It will eat the infection and crawl back out.

- Cover the ear with a hot rag and lie with that side of the head down.

- Blow warm air from a hairdryer into a sore ear to cure an earache.

- Put corn syrup on a cotton ball and place it in the ear for a couple of hours.

- Wrap a hot iron in a clean towel, lay the sore ear down and rest on the towel until it cools.

- Put a drop of sweet oil in each ear occasionally to help soften wax so it will work its way out of the ear more easily.

- Heat a thick dinner plate, wrap it in a towel and hold it on a sore ear.

- Mince some garlic cloves and let the small pieces marinate in olive oil for a day. Pour the mixture into the sore ear and it will cure an ear infection.

- Heat some urine in a teaspoon. Pour it in the sore ear. Lay with that ear turned up for about half an hour, then let the urine run back out.

- Drink sassafras tea and put some of it in your ear while it is still warm.
- Take the kernel out of a peach stone. Beat it up and put it in warm water. Put a drop of the water in the sore ear.
- Rub butter in a sore ear.

energy

- For energy, drink a little ginseng tea every day.
- A solid night of sleep (eight hours) will let your body rest and heal itself so that you have enough energy to get you through the next day.
- Drink plenty of water instead of other drinks.

eyes

- For healthy eyes, eat lots of carrots.
- Drink carrot juice to improve eye sight.
- For tired eyes, wash them in cold water several times a day.
- For puffy eyes, place slices of fresh cucumbers over the eyes.
- For tired or swollen eyes, lie down and place a thin slice of fresh potato over each eye.
- For eye infection, crush enough bedbugs to make a drop of liquid. Mix this with human milk and put a drop in the sore eye every night at bed time until the eye is cured.
- For dirt or grit in the eye, place one drop of fresh cream in the corner of each eye before bedtime.
- For dirt or grit in the eye, or to help clear infection, put a flax seed in the corner of each eye before you go to sleep.
- For a black eye, lay a fresh steak over the eye to reduce bruising.
- If you have an eye infection, hold a piece of half cooked onion on the eye and it will draw out the infection.

Maggie Harris

59

- When your eyes are mildly bothering you, cut limbs of a sassafras large enough to split. Take out the pulp inside. Sterilize water by boiling it. Cool the water. Put the pulp of the sassafras in a small amount of the boiled water. Soak it until the strength of the sassafras comes out in the water. Take a clean and sterilized cloth and strain the solution into a container that is sterilized. Wash your eyes with this solution. Be sure to see a doctor if it is anything more than tired eyes or irritation from allergies. This is meant to be only mild eyewash.

F

feet

- If you have tired or flat feet, fill a plastic water bottle part of the way up. Freeze it. When your feet hurt, take the bottle out and roll it back and forth under the bottom of your feet.
- If you step on a nail, take the nail and drive it into an oak tree. Your foot will heal.
- If you have cramps in your feet, turn your shoes upside down before you go to bed—even for a nap. When you get up, the cramps will be gone.
- To ease the pain of sore feet, soak them in hot salty water.
- Soak sore feet in hot water with Epsom Salts.
- To soothe sore feet soak your feet in vinegar water.
- Soak a towel in alcohol, and then wrap it around the sore foot or ankle.
- Mix salty water and vinegar together and soak your feet in it.

Lynch Mining Rescue Team

- To take swelling out of your feet, sleep on your back with your feet elevated higher than your head.
- Sulfur powder sprinkled in the shoes will keep disease away from the feet.
- Never wear the same socks unwashed, two days in a row.
- Always wear dry socks.

- For a bruise or a sprain in the feet, soak a brown paper bag in vinegar and wrap it around the affected area.

fever

- To calm a fever, boil two roots of wild ginger and drink the broth.
- Chew linden flowers to induce sweating if you have a fever.
- Suck on a lemon to reduce a fever.

George Hamlin holding Francis, Ada Hamlin, Henry Hensley, Edith Hamlin, others unidentified.

- Alcohol rubs bring down fever.
- Drink a hot toddy made of 1 tablespoon of ginger, the juice of one fresh lemon, ¼ cup of moonshine, and warm water to the top of a tumbler. Mix with a spoon. Hold your nose and drink it all down as quickly as possible.
- Take rabbit dung and boil it. Strain the water off and drink it. Repeat this every so often throughout the day until the fever breaks.
- For a mild fever, wrap up in a warm blanket and drink a cup of hot yarrow tea.
- Wrap slices of onions on the bottom of the feet (or inside a pair of white cotton socks) to draw out a fever overnight.
- Keep sipping on icy things to help cool a fever.
- Starve a fever, feed a cold.
- To get rid of fever in a child, wrap the child in warm blankets until they break out in a sweat. Once they start sweating, the fever will go away.
- Soak in a cold tub of water.
- Put cold compresses on the head.
- Strip the person down to their underwear and lay cold rags on them.
- Sit in front of the door and let a cool breeze blow over the feverish person.

- Soak in alternating hot water and cold water.
- Suck on ice chips until the fever comes down.
- Cut an onion in half and place it under the bed of a sick person to draw out their fever.

fever blister (see also **cold sore**)

- Put ear wax on a fever blister.
- Scrape a fresh corn cob to get the white pasty liquid that comes out after the kernels are cut away. Put that on the fever blister to help it heal.

flu

- Chew rabbit tobacco to get rid of the flu.
- Eat onions to ease symptoms of the flu.
- Sprinkle sulfur inside the soles of your shoes.
- Gather boneset. Put the leaves in a sack and put it in the sun to dry. When the leaves are dry, crush them and cook them in water. Strain the water and drink it.

food poisoning

- Eat lots of bread to help cure food poisoning, and drink lots of milk.
- Food poisoning or for a child having swallowed something dangerous make them drink warm grease.

freckles

- Mix lemon juice with buttermilk and put it on freckles to remove them.
- On May 1, gather early morning dew and wash your face in it. Your freckles will lighten up.
- Gather early morning dew, rub it on your face and repeat nine times, "Dew, dew, take my freckles and wear them on you!" Don't wash or rub your face until the next morning and your freckles should be gone.
- Wash your face in pickle juice.
- Cucumber juice will bleach freckles.
- Stay out of the sun if you don't want freckles!

G

gall bladder trouble

• Drink tea made from white oak bark.

general well being

• Take ginseng for general well being. It is believed by the Chinese to heal everything and is called "Man Root".

• Yellow Parilla is good for everything.

• Yellow oak bark makes a good tonic.

• Blood root is for general well being.

• Mix one part of sulfur and one part of lack strap molasses. Take a teaspoon full at bed time from time to time for general well being.

• Black cohosh is for general well being – especially for women.

• A common remedy for everything was white liniment.

• Wear an asiphidity bag around the neck to keep illness away.

• In the spring, for a general cleanse, drink bur vine tea or square root to cleanse the body of winter toxins.

• Take cod liver oil every day to stay healthy. Take 1 teaspoon full with one graham cracker every day for general health.

• Pennyroyal tea grows by the creek. It has a pleasant taste. Gather it by the root and hang it upside down to try. Make tea from the leaves or the root. A little sugar can be added.

• Red sassafras tea taken in the spring is a tonic for well being.

groundhog grease

• Groundhog grease is good to use for allergies. Just rub a little inside the nose and it will collect pollens or allergens from getting deep into the nose, sinuses, throat, and lungs.

Bessie Boggs, Sarah Boggs, Aunt Sadie (Sarah) — Bach-Noctor, KY

- Groundhog grease can also be given to babies with the croup. When the baby is choking on congestion, a little groundhog grease, given in small amounts at a time will loosen the congestion and the baby will throw up the congestion. It is a great help if you can't get a baby to the doctor.
- Groundhog grease is also very good for fungus such as athlete's feet. Cover the feet with groundhog grease and put socks on. Sleep with that on your feet. Keep the feet as dry as possible. Wash them daily and reapply groundhog grease on the feet daily with clean socks at night. If possible, grease the feet during the day and wear sandals so the air can get to them and help with the healing process. Usually the groundhog grease treatment will make a difference in the feet overnight.

growth
- Drink coffee if you want to stunt your growth.
- Every time you eat a banana, you will grow a tiny bit taller.

gums
- For sore gums, use golden seal (yellow root).
- Brush your teeth with baking soda if you want healthy gums.

H

hair
- Use a mixture of mayonnaise and egg on the hair as a weekly conditioner to give it shine and make it healthy.
- To get gum out of hair—put peanut butter on the hair and gum and gently rub it. The gum should slide out.
- Vinegar used in rinse water will help get rid of dandruff and some believe it will help prevent lice.
- To make hair shine, at least once a month, soak it in olive oil; wrap a towel around your head for about an hour or two, then wash thoroughly.
- Squeeze the juice of a lemon into the rinse water you are going to pour over your hair.

- To lighten hair, put lemon juice through your hair and sit in the sunshine for 30 minutes to an hour.
- For oily hair, massage lemon juice on your scalp.
- Rinse hair in beer to make it shine.
- Rub a little olive oil on the palms and work it into the ends of the hair to avoid split ends.

J.G. and Betty Hackler
Wallins Creek, KY

- Make a tea from the bark of an aspen tree and drink it.

headache

- Chew on oak bark to cure a headache.
- Eat a little salty dough.
- Take a hornets' nest and wet it up or wrap it in a wet rag. Put it on your head and it will stop a migraine headache.
- Mix cinnamon with water and rub it on your forehead to get rid of a headache.
- Chew fresh basil to stop a headache.
- Inhale basil oil to cure a migraine.
- Lay thin slices of raw onions on the forehead to ease a headache.
- Sleep with a pair of scissors under your pillow to cut the pain.
- Dampen a washcloth with rubbing alcohol and lay it lightly across the forehead to ease a headache.
- White willow bark chewed can help stop a headache or general pain.
- Get your hair cut on Good Friday and it will prevent you from getting headaches in the following year.
- Suck on peppermint or drink peppermint tea to relive a headache.
- Wear black walnut leaves in your hat.
- Massage the shoulders, working up the back to the base of the head to relieve a headache.

- Use cold compresses on the forehead or temple to cure a headache.
- Drink willow tea to relieve a headache.
- Gently massage the temples to relieve a headache.
- Sniff warm salt water.
- Sleep with a knife under your bed to cut the pain of a headache if you have one when you are going to bed at night.
- Hold something cold against the back of the neck and/or temples to get rid of a headache.
- Put ice on the web of skin between your thumb and forefinger to relieve a headache, or gently pinch that skin from the top and bottom.
- Boil a pot of onions. Hold your head over the steaming pot and breathe deeply to cure a headache.
- Hold an ice pack or ice cube on the back of the neck to cure a headache.

heart
- For a healthy heart eat lots of tomatoes.
- Eat your food with garlic cooked in to help lower your cholesterol and have a healthy heart.
- Eating lots of onions is good for your heart.
- To strengthen your heart, drink dandelion juice.
- To strengthen your heart, drink dandelion tea.
- Foxglove tea in very small doses will help cure heart trouble.

Blanton's Store —
Wallins Creek, KY — 1903

- Include a combination of garlic and fresh onions in your daily diet to help keep a healthy heart.

heartburn

- Drink a cup of warm water with a teaspoon of baking soda in it to relieve heartburn.
- Chew dogwood bark to relieve heartburn.
- Drink tea made from ginger root to help relieve heartburn.
- Take a teaspoon of honey mixed with cinnamon powder to relieve heartburn.
- Take a dose of sulfur from matches to relieve heartburn.
- Drink milk and eat dry crackers.

hiccups

- To cure hiccups, eat a tablespoon of peanut butter.
- To cure hiccups, eat a teaspoon of dry, granulated sugar.
- A teaspoon of sugar under the tongue will cure hiccups.
- Sneak up on the person who has hiccups and grab them in the ribs and holler real loud. That will scare the hiccups right out of them.
- Sip nine sips of water out of the back side of a teacup without spilling a single drop and you will be cured.
- Massage your eyelids gently until the hiccups stop.
- Hold your breath while you drink a whole glass of water.
- Hold your breath and pinch your nose for one full minute and your hiccups will be gone.
- Drink warm milk to cure hiccups.
- Have the person with the hiccups hold their arms above their head while you hold a glass of water and make them drink every drop without taking a breath.
- Gently massage your temples to make hiccups stop.
- Get one drink of water. Swallow it. Hold your breath and count until 10.
- Go outside with a cold glass of water and let the wind blow in your face while you drink the whole glass of water.

- Stand on your head and try to swallow a drink of water.
- Stand on our head for thirty seconds to cure hiccups.
- Blow up a paper bag and burst it. That will get rid of the hiccups.
- To cure hiccups, drink nine sips of water from a teacup without breathing in between.
- Hold a teaspoon of sugar in your mouth and let it dissolve slowly to cure hiccups.
- Take a teaspoon of sugarcane sugar to cure hiccups.
- Breathe in a paper bag to cure the hiccups.
- Take three big gulps of any carbonated drink (pop) and swallow it all without breathing. Your hiccups will be gone!
- Take a teaspoon of hot sauce to get rid of hiccups.
- Recite this rhyme, and then drink nine sips of water: He-cup, teacup, Nine sips of water out of a teacup will cure the hiccups.
- Hold your nose closed and your mouth for one minute completely before you breathe again. The hiccups will be gone.
- When a baby has hiccups, don't fret. It just means the child is growing.

hickey
- Put toothpaste on the bruised area.
- Hold ice on the bruised area.
- Freeze a spoon and tap the bruise with the bowl of the spoon to help the blood dissipate. Repeat as needed.

high blood pressure
- Drink coffee to help with blood pressure.
- Avoid drinking coffee or caffeine drinks to avoid high blood pressure.
- Eat dandelion greens to help bring down high blood pressure.

hives
- Give a baby a little catnip tea to cure hives.
- Eat gingerbread to cure hives.
- Boil a bunch of catnip in water, strain and drink.

infection

- To help fight infection, use olive oil on the infected area.

- Moss makes a good poultice to draw out infection.

inflammation

- Use chamomile flowers to make a tea in order to reduce inflammation.

Begley Hall and Irvina Soular

- Slice a fresh onion. Heat the slice slightly in a skillet or in a microwave. Lay the onion on the inflamed joint or sore and it will draw the infection out. There may be puss that will come to the surface. Changing the onion to a fresh slice, freshly heated as needed, will draw the inflammation out.

itch

- Ivy root tea and tallow mixed to a paste and applied to an itchy spot will bring relief.

- Laurel root boiled in water to make a thick oozy consistency can be put on any type of itching skin.

- To get rid of the seven year itch, mix hog grease and sulfur together and cover the itchy skin every day for seven days. Make sure to bathe and change to clean clothes every day before applying the mixture.

joints

- Spray WD-40 on sore joints to ease arthritis pain.

K

kidneys

- To help with kidney problems, use Queen of the Meadow to make a tea and drink a cup every day until feeling better.

- Make a tea from fresh blueberries or raspberries. Drink the tea for a few days.

Sampson, Sr. and James Curry

- Drink cranberry juice.
- Drink blackberry juice made from fresh blackberries or strain the juice from canned blackberries and drink a cup a day until you are feeling better.
- Drink yellow root tea.
- Boil watermelon seeds and drink the strained liquid.
- Mix one tablespoon of honey with one fourth cup of cider vinegar and fill the rest of the glass with warm water. Mix

until the honey is dissolved. Drink the whole glass. Do this once a day as needed until feeling better.

L

leg cramps

- To relieve a leg cramp, rub apple cider vinegar on the muscle.
- Eat a banana every day to help stop leg cramps.
- Elevate the legs while sleeping.
- Sleep with a pillow between the knees.
- Pinch your upper lip until the leg cramp stops.

lice

- Coat your head in mayonnaise overnight.
- Soak your head for a few hours in sassafras oil.
- Soak your head in Clorox thoroughly, and let set a few minutes. Then wash your hair completely and remove all Clorox. The lice and nits will be dead.
- Some say the only way to be completely rid of lice is to be completely rid of hair. Shave your head.
- Rub salt into your scalp.

- Soak your hair in peroxide and grease overnight. (Wrap your head in a towel.) Wash it out the next morning.
- Soak your hair in tomato juice.
- Strip out all the live lice with a fine toothed comb. Separate the hair into small strips and pull the nits off with your fingernails. Pop the nits between your fingernails to make sure they can't hatch.
- Lay your clothes on an ant hill and leave them over night to make sure there are no lice or nits in your clothing.
- Put freshly squashed tomatoes all over your hair. Let this set for a while, and then wash it all out.
- Soak your head in olive oil and wrap in a hot towel for two hours. Then pour warm vinegar all through the hair, wring it out and wrap again in a hot towel for two hours. Wash thoroughly. Repeat every other day for ten days.
- The best way to treat lice is not to get them in the first place! Never wear someone else's hat, headband, earphones, or hoodie. Never borrow someone else's comb or brush!
- Soak your head with hair spray and wrap your head in Saran Wrap for an hour. Wash thoroughly.
- Rinse your hair in perfume to keep lice away.
- Rinse your hair in vinegar water every time after you shampoo.
- Pour whiskey on your scalp.
- Soak your head in coal oil for ten minutes, and then wash thoroughly.
- Spray DDT on the head of a lice infected person. (This is extremely dangerous and was taken off the market.)
- Soak the head and hair of a lice infected person in coal oil. Keep it covered for a couple of hours. (very dangerous)

liver

- Eat turnips to cleanse the liver.
- Take a good dose of castor oil once a week to cleanse the liver.

Opal Hopkins and Friends

71

M

measles

- Drinking sassafras tea will help the measles break out.

- One teaspoon of liquor and sugar makes measles break out.

- Sit in a hot tub of water to make measles break out.

- Take a bath in Epson salt water to keep measles from itching.

- Soak a towel in cool Epson salt water and lay it over the person's skin that has measles to ease the itching.

- To avoid getting the measles, burn some cornmeal and carry it in a little pouch around the neck.

menstrual cramps

- Drink ginger tea for cramps. Make any kind of tea you like and while it is hot, stir in as much ginger as you can stand to drink. It will take care of the cramps quickly.

migraine headaches

- For a migraine, smell of camphor oil.

- To cure a migraine, lie down in a dark room on your back and put a cold washcloth over your face. There should be no noise, light or interruptions. Lay as still as possible until the headache passes.

- Eat warm chicken noodle soup.

- Take two crushed aspirin, drink a small bottled coke, and eat some chocolate. Lay down (if possible) and the migraine will ease off.

- Migraines are marked by flashing lights ahead of the headache. When the lights start flashing before your eyes, immediately take a cure. Don't wait until the pain sets in.

- Take a hornet's nest and wet it or wrap it in a rag. Lie down and put it on your head and keep it there until the headache goes away.

- Lay down flat of your back on the bed. Stack all of your pillows under your feet and lay still. Your headache will go away.

- Sniff warm or cold salt water up your nose a little bit at a time.

mosquito bites

- Put a hot rag on a mosquito bite.
- A paste of flour and water on a mosquito bite will relieve the itch.
- Spray salt water on a mosquito bite, as needed.
- Rub alcohol or vinegar on a mosquito bite.

William and Teathia Belcher

- Calamine lotion will take the itch out of a mosquito bite.
- Paint a mosquito bite with shoe polish to relieve the itch.
- Use aloe juice on a mosquito bite to take the swelling out.
- Eat garlic every day and you won't have to worry about mosquitoes biting in the first place!

motion sickness

- Drink ginger tea before traveling to prevent motion sickness.
- Wear a brown paper bag under your clothes, next to the skin of your chest to prevent motion sickness.
- Ginger root helps with motion sickness.

mouth sores

- Rinse your mouth out with salt water.
- Gargle with peroxide followed by a salt water gargle.
- Suck on ice chips. Try to let them melt on the sore.
- Goldenseal root is good as a mouthwash for canker sores.
- Chew yellow root to cure a mouth sore.
- Gargle salt water and paint the sore with salt water to help it dry up.

mumps

- To avoid getting the mumps if you have been exposed, tie a black sock around your neck.
- If a boy gets the mumps, tie a red sock around his waist to keep the mumps from falling on him to his male parts.

- If a child has the mumps, they should not be allowed to play or jump. This can cause the mumps to fall on them and affect their reproductive parts.

muscle aches

- Fill a sock part of the way full with uncooked rice. Heat it in the microwave until the rice and sock are very warm. Hold it on the sore muscle. It will help relieve pain.
- Soak a warm washcloth in vinegar and place it on the sore muscle to relieve pain.
- Heat a moist towel in the microwave and place it on the sore muscle to relieve pain.
- Soak in a hot bath of Epsom salts.

N

nail fungus

- Put tea tree oil on the infected nails.
- Soak nails in Epsom salts daily.
- After a hot bath, butt nails back and put Vicks Vapor Rub on the infected nails daily.

neck pain

- Stand with the sun shining on the back of the neck. This will ease the pain.
- Massage the shoulders to relieve neck pain.

Wash and Patty (Hensley) Fee

- Find a spot where an animal has rubbed up against a piece of wood—like a fence or the corner of the barn. Sub your neck in that same place and your pain will go away.
- Sleep on your back without a pillow.

nerves

- Drink tea made from chamomile flowers to treat nervousness or shock.

Monroe Miller and Nelly McGregory Miller

Ken, Virgie, and Carolyn Blanton—Wallins, KY

- Drink warm milk to help soothe nerves.
- Soak feet in warm salt water to help sooth nerves.
- Lay in a dark, silent room with a warm towel on the forehead for fifteen minutes to help calm nerves.
- Lay on your back and take deep, slow breaths for five minutes
- Take a hot soapy bath before bedtime to help calm nerves after a hectic day

nose bleed

- Wear a Yankee dime around your neck to cure nose bleeds.
- Tear a piece of brown paper from a grocery bag and place it inside your mouth between your top lip and your gum and leave it there until the nosebleed stops.
- Hold a dime on our upper lip directly under your nose with slight pressure.
- For two weeks, every day in a row, pour a bucket of cold water over the person's head that has severe nosebleeds. At the end of the two weeks, they should be cured.
- Have someone quote to the person with the nosebleed Ezekiel 16:6: And when I passed by thee, and saw thee polluted in thine own blood, I said unto thee, "When thou was in thy blood, Live;" Yea, I said unto thee," when thou wast in thy blood, Live."

P

Dr. George Calloway

pain

- To relieve pain, drink some black tea.
- Chew on willow bark.
- Cut an onion in half and place it under a person's bed to draw out pain.
- If you have pain at night, sleep with a knife under your pillow, under your mattress, or under the bed.
- If you have pain in the bed, sleep with an axe under the bed.

pigs

- If you want a female pig to lose her babies, feed her dogwood berries.

pimple

- To help a pimple go away faster, put milk on it and let it dry.
- Daily wash your face with soap and warm water, but rinse with ice water to avoid pimples.
- Wash your face with soap and ice water to avoid pimples.
- To get rid of a pimple(s), put one fourth cup of salt into a pot of water. Heat the water until it is boiling. Hold a towel over your head above the boiling water to form a tent. Let the steam from the salt water cover your face. Keep your face over the steam, remove it from the heat (turn the heat off) and keep your face over the steam until the water has cooled enough to stop producing steam.
- Mix molasses with sulfur and paint it on a pimple.
- Sift oatmeal through a sifter. Keep the part that makes it through the sifter. Make a paste from this part and use it as a facial to dry up pimples and clean out pores.
- To dry up a pimple, put toothpaste on it overnight or mustard.
- To draw a pimple to a head, put the inside of a raisin over the pimple and cover it with a bandage overnight.
- Take the inside skin of an egg and put it over a pimple, and then covers it with a bandage to draw out the pimple.

- Make a salt paste and put on a pimple several times a day.
- Rub jewel weed on a pimple to help relieve the pain.
- Use raw egg whites on a pimple.
- Put pig fat on a pimple.
- Brush a pimple until it is raw, and then wash it with hot soapy water, followed by alcohol.
- Take baking soda, bay leaves, and salt. Crunch the leaves so fine they are almost powder. Mix the ingredients together and add a little water, enough to form a paste. Put it on your face for 10 minutes, and then wash it off.
- Put toothpaste on a pimple overnight.
- Put black electrical tape over a bad pimple overnight. It will draw it to a head by the next morning.

pneumonia

- Take a teaspoon of kerosene mixed with sugar to cure pneumonia.
- Make a mustard plaster, warm it, and place one on the back and one on the chest of the patient.
- Make a poultice of cooked onions to go on the patient's chest and back. They should start coughing up the mucus in a few hours. Change the poultice before it gets cold.

Billy Mac Conatser, Eddie Bear Stephens

William, Marie, Freeman, Christine, Florence, Bernice, Esther, Thelma, Danny Ray, and Geneva Fowler

- Drink birch tea to help cure pneumonia.
- In a young child, lay the child over your knees or over a shoulder and pat firmly but gently on the child's back until they begin to spit up the congestion. Repeat.
- Rub goose grease all over the chest and cove r with a warm flannel rag to break up congestion.

poison

- A mixture of coal oil, turpentine, and melted lard will make a person vomit who has eaten poison.
- Humans: Drink buttermilk and warmed lard mixed together. Continue until the person begins to vomit. They will vomit out the poison.
- Animals: Feed the animals egg yolks.

poison ivy

- If you know you've been exposed to poison ivy, go straight home, get out of the clothes you were wearing, and take a hot soapy bath. Make sure the clothes are washed in hot water and be careful when handling them when you first take them off.
- If you know for sure that you have been exposed to poison ivy, you can rinse your skin with cold water and Clorox.
- Use the juice from an aloe plant on poison ivy to help it go away.
- Bathe in oatmeal to take the itch out of poison ivy.
- Take a bath in hot baking soda water to cure poison ivy.

- Take a bath in cold Clorox water to kill out poison ivy.
- Rub fresh watermelon rind over poison ivy.
- Make a paste of oatmeal and spread it on poison ivy to dry it up and make it go away.
- Rub jewel weed on poison ivy to take the itch out.

Nancy and Bill Conatser, Granny Bryant, Mindy (Tom) Shelly

Top Row: Wye Wilder, Jim Warf, Robert Long. Second Row: Robert Giles, Garrett Giles, Ulright Cottrell. Bottom Row: Eck Long, John Harber, George Martin

- Rub the juice of forget-me-not flowers on poison ivy rash to make it go away.
- Rub the juice of touch-me-not flowers on poison ivy to relieve the itch.
- Bathe the irritated area of poison ivy in Clorox to kill the poison ivy.
- If you know you've touched poison ivy, wash with strong lye soap.
- Velvet weed is good to put on poison ivy.
- Waterweed or butterfly weed is good to put on poison ivy.
- Rub ragweed on poison ivy.
- Fill a bathtub full of cold water. Add ginger and soak for 30 minutes.
- Rub salt on the inflamed area to help dry up poison ivy.
- Use a mixture of buttermilk, vinegar, and salt on poison ivy to draw out the itch.
- Bathe in salt and soda water.
- Fry okra in a skillet. Take the thick stuff that come out of the okra and let it cool. Then put it on the poison ivy to make it go away.
- Take the juice from planton and rub on poison ivy.
- Take touch-me-nots and burst them over a sheet. Save the seeds. Mash the seeds up and rub them on the poison ivy and it will go away.
- Take the oozy white liquid out of a milkweed plant and put it on the poison ivy.

poison oak
- Rub poke root on poison oak. Use similar cures as poison ivy.

R

rash

- Sprinkle cornstarch on a rash just like you would sprinkle baby powder.
- Make a paste from oats and spread it over the rash to help it go away.
- Burdock root will help cure a rash.
- Boil cornstarch in water. When it cools down, rub it on a rash to help take the itch out.
- Boil oatmeal in saltwater, and then smooth the liquid over a rash.
- Urinate on a rash.

ringworm

- Cover the ringworm circle with grease and sulfur and cover it with a bandage. Repeat daily until it is gone.
- Take ashes and spit in them to make a paste. Rub this on the ringworm sore and cover it. Do this daily until the ringworm is gone.
- Place chewed tobacco over the ringworm and bandage it up. Do this daily until the ringworm goes away.

S

shingles

- Rub blackened blood on the shingles.
- Sprinkle cornstarch on the shingles.
- Rub vinegar on the shingles.
- Make a paste of oatmeal, salt, and warm water to spread over shingles.
- Use lard and sulfur mixture to rub on the shingles.
- Rub the blood of a black chicken on shingles.

sinus problems

- Chew horsemint to clear the sinuses.
- Eat horse radish for sinusitis.
- Chew on fresh honeycomb to clear sinuses.

- Eat lots of onions to avoid sinus problems.
- Put one drop of skunk oil under the nose to clear sinus problems.

skin problems

- Crushed leaves of chickweed will help itchy skin.
- Put honey on a blemish to help it heal faster.
- Marigold blooms soaked in olive oil for a week in a sunny window, shaken from time to time, can be used to treat minor skin irritations or abrasions.
- Boil ivy root down until it makes a thick fluid. Mix with lard. Rub on skin irritations.
- A lotion made with buckeye sap will heal a sore.
- For infections of the skin that have festered and show yellow puss you can take the yolk of one egg and mix enough salt in it to make a paste. Cover the infected sore with the paste and wrap it securely. It only takes a small amount of this paste to cover a sore. The rest can be covered and stored in the refrigerator to use until the sore is healed. The next morning, take off the poultice and wash the sore in warm salt water. If all the puss is not gone, repeat the process again as many days as needed until the puss is gone and the sore is dried up. Once the puss is gone, do not cover up the sore.

skunk spray

- To remove the stink of skunk spray, bathe in tomato juice.

sleep

- Take a hot bath with mint leaves to help you sleep well.
- Make a potpourri out of dried lilacs and put them above your bed to make you sleep well.
- Drink chamomile tea before bed time to help get a good night's sleep.

smallpox sores

- Bathe smallpox sores in arrow root.

Unidentified McCreary County, KY

snake bite

- Soak a snake bite in moonshine to draw the poison out.
- Take the pulp inside of a cactus plant and make a poultice to go over a snake bite.
- Poke the holes of the bite with a hot object such as the end of a clothes hanger, then suck out the poison and spit it out.
- Submerge the snake bite in kerosene to draw the poison out.
- Take a freshly killed chicken breast and hold it on a snake bite to draw the poison out.
- Kill a chicken. Lay a piece of the fresh chicken meat over the snake bite. It will draw out the poison.
- Cut "X" marks on top of the fang marks. Suck out the poison or use an empty plastic bottle to suck it out. Squeeze all air out of the plastic bottle, then place the opening over the wound and squeeze the bottle again to form suction.
- Pack a snake bite in ice and get to the hospital as fast as possible.
- Pack a snake bite in mud until you can get help.
- Pack a snake bite in fresh cow dung to draw the poison out.
- Take a freshly killed deer heart or liver and hold it on a new snake bite to draw out the poison.
- Lay salt pork or fat back on a snake bite to draw the poison out.

- Split open a cactus and put the juicy part of the cactus over the snakebite to draw out the poison.
- Put chewed tobacco on a snake bite to draw the poison out.
- Pour gunpowder on a snake bite.
- Drink cockle burr milk for a snake bite.
- Boil cockle burr plant, root and all, until it cooks down to a thick liquid. Spoon off the syrup and add it to a glass of milk. Drink the whole thing down.
- Pack the bite in a hot salt poultice.

Unidentified Church Service

sore

- A peach poultice on a wound will help it heal.
- If you have a sore that won't heal, let your dog lick it. It will heal faster.
- Sap from the Gilly Bam tree will cure a sore. (also called Balm of Gilead bush)
- Place the inside skin of an egg on a fresh sore to help it heal faster.
- Rub a piece of salty meat on a sore and it will heal faster.
- To heal a sore, cover it with brown sugar, and then place a bandage over it. Change it daily until the sore is healed.
- Use heartleaf to make a salve for sores.

sore throat

- Gargle hot salty water at least three times a day – as hot and as salty as you can stand it to cure a sore throat.
- Golden seal or yellow root is good for a sore throat.
- Dissolve aspirin in hot water, add salt, stir, and use for a gargle to stop sore throat.
- Drink warm milk and honey.
- Drop camphor on sugar in a teaspoon until the sugar is soaked. Swallow.
- Gargle hot vinegar (as hot as you can stand it, but not hot enough to burn).
- Gargle pickle juice from a freshly opened jar of pickles.
- Suck on rock candy or horehound candy.
- Let a teaspoon of honey melt in your mouth and swallow a little bit at a time to cure a sore throat.
- Boil onions with honey or molasses and take it a teaspoon at a time, as needed, to ease a sore throat.
- Boil yellow root and gargle the water to cure a sore throat.
- Put lard on a chicken feather and paint the back of your throat with it.
- Let someone who has never seen their father blow cigarette smoke in the mouth of the person with a sore throat.

- In a bottle, mix water, pepper, and vinegar. Shake it well. Heat it and drink it to take away a sore throat.
- Gargle a mixture of hot water, salt, and baking soda.
- Wear a dirty sock around your neck when you go to bed. (your own sock that you wore that day)
- Dissolve two aspirins and two tablespoons of salt in a teacup of hot water. Gargle with this mixture until you have used the whole teacup. Swallow the last mouth full of the solution.
- Put one drop of camphor on a sugar lump and suck on it.
- Gargle a mixture of water and peroxide. Make sure you rinse your mouth thoroughly when you are done and do not swallow any of the mixture.
- Gargle heated pickle juice.
- Take a teaspoon of hot syrup to ease a sore throat.
- To treat hoarseness, using the following recipe:
    1 whole onion diced
    3–4 tablespoons of sugar
    1 cup of hot (boiling) water
Mix all the ingredients together and let them cool. Take 1 tablespoon from the mixture. It can be taken every three hours as needed.

spinal meningitis
- To ward off spinal meningitis, dip a string in aciphidity and tie one around the neck of every child in the family.

splinters
- If you get a splinter that won't come out, cover it with black electrical tape. Leave the tape on overnight. By the next morning, the splinter will come out with the tape when you pull it off.
- If you are going to try to pick a splinter out with a needle, make sure the needle has been cleaned with alcohol or burned over a candle before using it on the splinter.
- Cleanse the spot thoroughly after removing a splinter.
- Tweezers are best to get a splinter out. Pull it in the opposite direction of how it went in.

Sarah Boggs   *Maggie Strunk*
Roark Branch, KY   *Marshes Siding, KY*

sprain

- Soak a brown paper bag in vinegar and wrap it around the sprained joint to take down the swelling and draw out the soreness and/or bruise.
- Bathe a sprained ankle in vinegar, and then sleep with a sock over it.
- Soak a mud dauber's nest in vinegar until it has dissolved enough to make a pasty substance. Smear it over the sprain and wrap it in a bandage. It will draw out the swelling, pain, and discoloration.
- Soak a sprain in a vinegar bath.
- Put raw meat on a sprain to pull the swelling and bruising out.

stinging nettle

- Rub jewel weed on the welts made by stinging nettle.

stings (see also **bee stings**)

- Use a flat edge, like the edge of a credit card, to scrape a stinger out of a wasper sting or a bee sting as soon as it happens. It won't hurt nearly as bad or swell up as much.
- Wet tobacco is good on any type of sting.
- Cut a fresh clove of garlic and rub it on any sting to keep the swelling from spreading and relieve the pain.

stomach ache (see also **upset stomach**)

- Dust dry flour over the stomach and abdomen.
- Take oil of peppermint, sugar, and hot water mixed together for the relief of a stomach ache.
- Chew sweet flag flowers to help a stomach ache.
- Chew on a peppermint plant to soothe a sick stomach.
- Suck a lemon to help settle a sour stomach.
- Drink V-8 juice or tomato juice with lemon in it to settle a sour stomach.
- Drink some sauerkraut juice to ease a stomach ache.
- Drink catnip tea to help with stomach problems.
- A couple of drops of turpentine in a teaspoon of water will help relieve a stomach ache.
- Cut a small locket of hair from the side of your head that matches the side where the stomach pain is. Throw it over that shoulder in the light of a full moon and the pain will go away.
- Lie on your back and gently rub your stomach.
- Boil tender poke shoots in water. Strain off the liquid and separate it from the rest. Let it cool a little. Drink the liquid to soothe a stomach ache.
- Drink warmed milk to help relieve a stomach ache.

stomach flu

- Make bur vine tea from the weed vine. Boil it into a tea and store it. If a person gets the stomach flu, make them drink it. It will make

Lloyd and Joshua Cochran

them throw up, and they will soon be better. It can also work for someone who has swallowed something poisonous.

sty

- If you have a sty, rub a small round stone on the sty and throw it in a crossroads. Say the following, "Sty, sty, on my eye, go to the next stranger that passes by." The next person you do not know who passes that way will get your sty and yours will go away.

- A sty may come up on your eye if you have deliberately not told the truth to someone. In order to be free of the sty, you must go to that person and tell them the truth, and set things right. Your sty will go away.

stuttering

- If a child stutters, make him/her suck on chicken gizzard to take the stuttering away.

sunburn

- Use aloe plant juice on sunburn to ease the pain and speed healing.
- Mix up laundry starch very thick and put it on sunburn.
- Place thin Irish potato slices over the sunburn until it cools.
- Put vinegar on a sunburn.
- Make a strong tea with sage leaves and spread the tea on the sunburn.
- Cucumber juice mixed with cow's cream will soothe sunburn.

swelling or sprain

- Soak a brown paper bag in vinegar to draw swelling out.
- Put fresh cucumber slices on a swollen area to reduce the swelling.
- Fresh tomato slices placed over a swollen area will help take the swelling out.
- A poultice of meal and water will bring down swelling.
- Potato slices over a sprain or swelling will help draw the pain and the swelling out of the injury.
- Fresh slices of yellow squash will draw out swelling.
- Zucchini peelings will draw out swelling.

T

teeth

- To have a thorough brushing and whiten your teeth, use a mixture of salt and baking soda on your toothbrush.
- Use the juice of bloodroot as toothpaste or as a mouthwash.
- If you have a tooth pulled, make sure to swish warm salt water in the hole every day until it heals (may need several times a day).
- If you can't find your toothpaste, make a past of baking soda and water on your toothbrush to clean them.
- You can make a toothbrush out of a small birth tree twig.
- Every so often, use a clean rough washcloth with toothpaste, baking soda, or salt on it and go around the front of each tooth and the back of each tooth, washing it thoroughly up to the gum line. This will keep your teeth cleaner and whiter.

teething

- Rub chamomile on a baby's gums to help relieve teething pain.
- Squash nine red ants and rub them on the baby's gums.
- Kill nine wood lice and smash them into pulp. Rub this on the baby's gums.
- Take nine hairs from the child's father and put them in a bag to be worn around the neck.
- Rub a minnow on a baby's gums to help with teething pain.
- Rub vanilla extract on a baby's gums to ease the pain of teething.
- Give a teething baby Creeping Charlie tea.
- Let the baby wear a dime on a string or in a pouch around its neck to help with teething.

thrush mouth

- Have a person whose father died before they were born blow into the mouth of a person who has thrush to cure thrush mouth.
- If someone is the seventh child of a seventh child, they can blow into a person's mouth that has thrush and it will go away.

First Crew to build railroad tracks in Kentucky at Wallins Creek

- The seventh son of a seventh son can blow in the mouth of a person with thrush and it will vanish.

thumb

- If you mash your thumb with a hammer, put toothpaste on it to ease the pain.

tick

- Soak the tick in alcohol until it lets go. Then burn the tick.
- Cover a tick in Vaseline. It will let go, then you can remove it.
- Never pull a tick out with tweezers. The head may be attached under the skin and cause problems later.
- Cover a tick in liquid soap. It will let go and back its head out so you can remove the whole thing with tweezers. This is especially good to use in hard to get to areas on humans such as the arm pit.
- Put a piece of cardboard under the tick. Light a match and touch the tick. It will let go at the first burn.
- Put vinegar on the tick and swirl the flame from a cigarette lighter around the tick in a circle without ever getting close enough to touch your skin. The tick will let go.
- Cover a tick with lard and the skin all around the tick. It will let go.
- Put a drop of turpentine on a tick. It will let go quickly. Be ready to pick it up with tweezers.
- If you pull a tick off that has been embedded in your skin, make sure to see a doctor and take the body of the tick with you in a baggie. The head may still be embedded under your skin and can still cause complications. The doctor can remove it and tell what type of tick it was.

toenails

- For an ingrown toenail, soak it nightly in salt water.
- For an ingrown toenail, cut a "v" in the center of the top edge of the nail. The ingrown part of the nail will grow out.
- For fungus nails, wash your feet nightly and apply Vicks Vapor Rub to your feet, especially around and under the toenails. Sleep in clean white socks over the Vapor Rub.
- Pee on infected toenails to help dry up the infection.
- Turpentine on an infected toenail will help dry it up.
- Rub a lizard liver on an ingrown toenail.
- To lift an ingrown toenail without damaging the toe or the rest of the nail, work a piece of string, yarn, or dental floss under the ingrown section and "lift" it out of the sore spot. Pour it full of peroxide followed by alcohol.
- Pack an ingrown toenail in salt until it dries up.
- Some people say to work a thick piece of yarn under the corner of an ingrown toenail and cut the section to leave it there under the toenail. It will help the toenail grow up and out of the skin and will absorb whatever medicine you put on the toe and take it under the toenail to do the most good.
- Never cut your toenails in a round shape if you want to avoid ingrown toenails. They should be cut square and filed straight across.

toothache

- Blow tobacco smoke onto the bad tooth.
- Take anise to relieve a toothache.
- Make a tea from the bark of a yellow oak. Get the water of the tea good and hot. Swish the tea in your mouth and spit it out. Hold the tea in your mouth — especially where the sore tooth is, and then spit it out.
- Rub whiskey on the gum of a sore tooth to ease pain.
- Put nutmeg on a toothache.
- If a tooth is hollow, catch a red ant and put it in the hole. It will sting the tooth and numb the pain.

- Let an aspirin dissolve in your mouth on a bad tooth to take away the pain.
- Put drops of vanilla extract on a sore gum or sore tooth to ease the pain.
- If you trim your fingernails or toenails on a Saturday, you will not have a toothache the following week.
- If you have a toothache, let someone blow smoke into your mouth. Any kind of smoke will do.
- Rub cayenne or ground poppy on a sore tooth.
- If you can see a hole in a tooth that is hurting or if you've lost a filling, fill the whole with bee's wax from the honeycomb (without the honey).
- Put moonshine or whiskey directly on the sore tooth and gum as needed to ease the pain.
- Stick a cotton ball over the sore tooth, between the tooth and gum and leave it there. It will ease the pain of a toothache.
- Put nutmeg in a cavity or on the infected gum.
- Hold a heated towel on the side of the face where there's a toothache.
- Hold ice in your left hand to stop a toothache.
- Drink green tea and swish it around the sore tooth to relieve a toothache.
- Mix liquid eugenol with zinc oxide and drop a couple of drops into a toothache.
- Burn some soda in a skillet until it is brown. Put it between the sore tooth and the cheek.

turpentine
- DO NOT PUT TURPENTINE ON THE HEAD!
- DO NOT DRINK TURPENTINE!
- Turpentine should be used only to rub on. You can put the bottle of turpentine to a snake bite. Turn the bottle up so the fluid is on the bite. Hold it there and let it draw out the poison. If possible, put ice on the bite. Be careful not to frostbite the snakebite area. Get to a doctor as soon as possible.

Judy, Bige, James Jr., Sampson Curry, unknown. Creech Pine Mountain—Down on Greasy, KY

- Turpentine is very good if you can't get to the doctor. For scrapes and scratches of metal, such as rusty wire or nails, wash the scratch or scrape with soap and water first. Then rub turpentine on and into the scratch or scrape. Leave the turpentine on the wound. It helps to keep blood poisoning from forming from the scrapes and scratches.

U

upset stomach
- Sip on clear citrus flavored sodas to help calm an upset stomach.
- Mix vinegar, soda water, and sugar in equal parts. Drink the mixture to cure an upset stomach.
- Squeeze a fresh lemon and get all the pulp out. Put salt in the juice and drink the juice.
- Take two drops of turpentine in one teaspoon of water and sugar.
- Eat warm soup to settle a stomach ache.
- Suck on peppermint to settle a stomach ache.
- Chew on a mint leaf to settle a sour stomach.
- Drink some carbonated drink or soda pop to ease a stomach ache.
- Take some ginger in water or make ginger tea to relieve an upset stomach. This will also help control vomiting.
- Sip on dill pickle juice until the stomach settles.
- Drink sassafras tea to help cure a stomach ache or chew on the bark of a young sassafras tree.
- Drink yellow root tea.

- Use slippery elm to make stomach medicine.
- Golden Seal or yellow root is good for the stomach.
- Teaberry is good for the stomach.
- Chew on horsemint to settle a sour stomach.
- Chew spearmint leaves to relieve a stomach ache.
- Mix a teaspoon of mustard in a warm cup of water and drink it down to cure a stomach ache.
- Melt a piece of peppermint stick in a cup of warm water and drink it cure an upset stomach.
- Drink peppermint tea to sooth an upset stomach.

urinary tract infections

- Drink cranberry juice or fresh blackberry juice.
- Use swamp roots for kidney problems.
- Drink tea made from arrowroot.

V

veins

- If you drink black coffee, it will turn your veins black.
- Spider veins are a sign of heart trouble.

W

warts

- Use a tiny drop of castor oil on the wart twice a day and tape it over.
- Rub a dead cat on a wart and the wart will disappear when you stop looking for it.
- If you buy one of the fake diamonds out of a machine and rub it on a wart and then throw it away where no one will find it, your wart will go away.

Margaret McDaniels

- Stick the hand with a wart in a paper bag. Take your hand out and tie the bag up and throw it away. Whoever finds the bag and unties it will get your warts.
- If you steal a dish rag that someone is using and bury it, when the dishrag rots, the wart will go away.
- If you use number one (urine) on the wart five times, it will go away.
- If you can find someone to buy the wart from you, it will go away.
- Find a pebble for each wart you have. Put them in a sack and tie it up. Hide the sack. If someone finds the sack and opens it, they will get the warts and yours will disappear.
- Take a stone for each wart you have and set them on the railroad track. When a train runs over them, the warts will go away.
- Burn the top of a wart with a cigarette. It will turn into a sore, and then fall off.
- Soak a wart in gasoline and it will fall off in a few days.
- Put black tape over a wart and leave it there for a week. When you take the tape off, the wart will be gone.
- Poke two holes in your wart with a needle and pour peroxide in the holes. The wart will dry up.
- If you cut a wart and make it bleed, it will go away.
- Cut a wart and make it bleed. Squeeze a drop of blood out of the wart onto a kernel of corn. Feed that kernel to a chicken. The wart will disappear.
- Rub an old bone on a wart. Throw it over your shoulder and don't look back. The wart will go away.
- Take a stick and cut a notch on the stick to number the same number of warts that you have. Throw the stick in the road. Whoever hits the stick will get the warts and your warts will go away.
- Take a penny and rub it on a wart seven times. Throw it down where people pass frequently. If someone stops to pick up the penny, they will also get the warts.
- Burn a wart with a match head.
- Put cooked oatmeal on a wart and bandage it up.

- Cut a wart with something until the blood comes out. Let the blood form a scab over the wart. When the scab comes off, the wart will be with it.

- Tie a fishing line around the wart real tight and leave it. Snip the ends of the line. It will cut the wart off.

- Wrap a long hair around a wart seven times tightly. What you forget about the hair and the wart, they will both be gone.

Nancy Coots and Children

- Get a hot needle and stick it all the way through a wart from side to side. The wart will go away on its own.

- Soak the wart in lemon juice, then put salt on it and cover it with a bandage overnight. Continue to do this until the wart is completely gone.

- Rub nine little stones on the warts and put the nine little stones in a match box. Put the match box in a creek where the water will run over it. The warts will wash away.

- Rub a cooked soup bean on a wart to make it go away every time you eat soup beans, until the wart is gone.

- If you have a wart on your hand, let your hand freeze on to something like ice or the inside of the refrigerator. It will make the wart go away.

- Take a quarter and color it with pencil lead. Put the colored side down on the wart and mash down hard and hold it for a while. The wart will go away.

weight loss
- Drink green tea to help with weight loss.

- Take a teaspoon of honey and a teaspoon of apple cider vinegar every day at least one time a day or after every meal.

- Squeeze the juice from half a lemon into a glass of water and drink it before every meal if you want to lose weight.

- Drink dill pickle juice every day.

- Eat a large dill pickle every day.

Tom Couch

- Use a dark tablecloth on the table where you are going to eat. It will cause you to eat less, therefore you will lose weight.
- To help lose weight, use a smaller plate than usual and no seconds!

whooping cough

- To cure whooping cough, swallow a minnow.
- Wear sheep dung in a pouch around the neck to ward off whooping cough.
- Take a hair from the sick person and put it in a dough ball. Feed it to the dog. If the dog eats the whole thing, the whooping cough will go away.
- Take a hair from the sick person and put it on a piece of bread outside their door or window in the moonlight. If an animal comes along and eats the bread with the hair, the hooping cough will go away.
- Take a hair from the sick person's head. Put it in food prepared for another person. If they eat the hair without discovering it, the whooping cough will go away.

worms

- If a child picks his/her nose, it is a sign of them having worms.
- Make a strong tea from walnut shells and/or pumpkin seeds. Take a teaspoon a day for a month.
- Make a tea from walnut shells. Drink a cup every day for a solid week.
- Take a teaspoon of sugar soaked in castor oil every day for a month to get rid of worms.
- Take a teaspoon of white granulated sugar or brown sugar. Soak in turpentine until the sugar is completely wet. Take it every day for 10 days to get rid of stomach worms. (turpentine is labeled as poisonous if taken internally)
- Boil walnut shells in water. Remove the shells. Take a tablespoon of the water every day for 10 days.
- Boil cabbage in a tub of water. Let the water cool down until it won't hurt the baby, then stick the baby in the tub with the cabbage and

the water and let the baby sit there and soak until the water is completely cool. This will not hurt the baby, but it will cause the worms to come out.

- If your lips are white, you probably have worms.
- Rub sugar and turpentine on the neck to keep worms from crawling up the throat and choking a child.

wounds

- To make a wound heal faster, put brown sugar on it, and then wrap it up.
- Soak a wound in salt water.
- Pack a wound in salt. It will keep down infection and dry up faster.
- A wet chew of a tobacco quid on a wound will draw out the infection.
- Lay a piece of fat bacon on a wound caused by a rusty nail and it will draw out the poison.
- Boil peach tree leaves for 30 – 40 minutes. Drain water off of the leaves. Put 1 teaspoon of salt in and thicken with cornmeal to make a poultice. Put it on the area. This also works for sores, nail punctures, or small wounds) and leave it overnight. This will take out the fever and swelling.

Y

yeast infection

- Eat yogurt to keep away yeast infections.
- If you get a yeast infection, use plain yogurt as a crème.
- Women can use a vinegar douche until a yeast infection is cleared up.

*Rudell, Price, Lena, and Irene Roark
Breathitt County, KY*

Wool Gathering   *Aunt Polly Day*
Pine Mountain, Kentucky

∾ **Rhymes** ∾

Cawood Family—Including Hiram, Green,
William and Carlo

Nursery rhymes were very popular in the United Kingdom during the 15th, 16th, and 17th centuries and began to find their way into print in different collections. However, most of them originated long before they were actually printed.

Some of the rhymes recorded in this section are identical to the original print versions and some of them have slight variations of wording. They were recorded as they were heard.

Apples

An apple a day will keep the doctor away.

Welch Folk Proverb, 1866

〰〰

Baa, Baa Black Sheep

Baa, baa, black sheep! Have you any wool?
Yes, sir. Yes, sir. Three bags full.
One for my master, one for my dame,
And one for the little girl who lives down the lane.

England, 1300s

〰〰

Baby Bunting

Don't cry Baby Bunting.
Daddy's gone a hunting
To find a brand new rabbit skin for to wrap sweet Baby Bunting in.

England, 1784

〰〰

Birdie, Birdie

Birdie, birdie in the sky
Dropping whitewash in my eye.
I'm no sissy. I won't cry!
Gee I'm glad cows don't fly!

Army Cadence

〰〰

Christmas Time's Coming

Christmas time's a coming and the goose is getting fat.
Please put a nickel in the old man's hat.
If you ain't got a nickel, a penny will do.
If you ain't got a penny, then God bless you!

An Old English Rhyme

〰〰

Church and Steeple

Here's the church, and here's the steeple.
Look inside at all the people!

Old English Rhyme

～♡～

Diddle, Diddle, Dumpling

Diddle, diddle dumpling, my son John,
Went to bed with his britches on;
One shoe off and one shoe on,
Diddle, diddle dumpling, my son John.

England, 1797 — First in print

～♡～

Duke of York

There was a Duke of York who had ten thousand men.
He marched them up to the top of the hill,
and then marched them down again!
When they were up, they were up, and
when they were down, they were down.
And when they were only half way up,
they were neither up nor down!

United Kingdom

～♡～

Early to Bed

Early to bed.
Early to rise.
Makes one healthy,
wealthy and wise.

Ben Franklin, 1735

*Gladys and Donald Kling
McCreary County, KY*

～♡～

Fatty, Fatty

Fatty, fatty,
2 x 4,
Can't get through the kitchen door!

Unable to find the origin

∽∘∾

Fools' Names

Fools' names and fools' faces
Always show up in public places.

Unable to find an origin

∽∘∾

Four and Twenty Blackbirds

Sing a song of sixpence, a pocket full of rye,
Four and twenty blackbirds baked in a pie.
When the pie was opened, the birds began to sing!
Now isn't that a pretty dish to set before the king?

London, 1744

∽∘∾

Georgie Porgie

Georgie Porgie, pudding and pie,
Kissed the girls and made them cry.
When the boys came out to play
Georgie Porgie ran away.

England, 1600s

∽∘∾

Good Night

Good night.
Sleep tight.
Don't let the bedbugs bite!

USA, 19th Century

∽∘∾

Hickory Dickory Dock

Hickory, dickory dock.
The mouse ran up the clock.
The clock struck one and
Down he ran!
Hickory, dickory, dock!

America, 1744

*Mildred Shelley
Marshes Siding, KY*

Hey, Diddle Diddle!

Hey, diddle diddle!
The cat's in the fiddle and the cow
jumped over the moon!
The little dog laughed to see such sport
And the dish ran away with the spoon!

London, England, 1765

Hiccups

Hiccup. Teacup.
Nine sups of water
Out of a teacup
Will cure the hiccups.

Unable to find origin

Humpity Dumpity

Humpity Dumpity sat on a wall.
Humpity Dumpity had a great fall.
All the king's horses,
And all the king's men
Couldn't put Humpity together again.

England, 1803

I See London

I see London.
I see France!
I see a hole in your under pants!

I see London.
I see France!
I see _____'s underpants! (fill in a name)

Unable to find the origin

Jack and Jill

Jack and Jill went up the hill
To fetch a pail of water.
Jack fell down and broke his crown and
Jill came tumbling after.

England, 1760s

Jack Be Nimble

Jack be Nimble,
Jack be quick.
Jack jump over
the candlestick!

16th Century England

*Tucker Child
Marshes Siding, KY*

Jack Sprat

Jack Sprat could eat no fat.
His wife could eat no lean.
And so betwixt them both, you see,
They licked the platter clean.

England, 1600s

Ladybug

Ladybug, ladybug, fly away home.
Your house is on fire and your children are gone.
There's only one left and that's little Anne
Who hid herself under a frying pan!

*England, 1600s (There is another version that uses the word
ladybird, ladybird instead of ladybug.)*

❧❦❧

Little Bo Peep

Little Bo Peep
Has lost her sheep.
She doesn't know where to find them!
Just leave them alone
And they'll come home,
Wagging their tails behind them!

England, 1805

❧❦❧

Little Boy Blue

Little Boy Blue, come and blow your horn.
The sheep are in the meadow and the cows are in the corn.
Where's the little boy who looks after the sheep?
He's under the haystack, fast asleep.
Who shall wake him?
No, not I, for if I do, he's sure to cry!

England, Early 1500s

❧❦❧

Little Hen

If I was a little hen,
Rooting in the yard;
If you were a little dog,
Would you bite me hard?

Unable to find the origin

❧❦❧

Little Jack Horner

Little Jack Horner sat in a corner eating his Christmas pie.
He stuck in his thumb and pulled out a plumb
And said, "What a good boy am I!"

England, around 1500

Little Miss Muffet

Little Miss Muffet sat on her tuffet eating her curs and whey.
Along came a spider and sat down beside her.
He frightened Miss Muffet away.

England, 1805

London Bridge

London bridge is falling down, falling down, falling down.
London bridge is falling down, my fair lady.
Take the keys and lock her up, lock her up, lock her up.
Take the keys and lock her up, my fair lady.

England, 1800s — origin uncertain

Blane Sharp, Anna, Maggie, Mary —
Back Row Manda and Mancie
McCreary Co., KY

Mary Had a Little Lamb

Mary had a little lamb. Its fleece was white as snow.
And everywhere that Mary went, the lamb was sure to go.
He followed her to school one day, which was against the rule.
It made the children laugh and play, to see a lamb at school!

Boston, 1830

❧

Mary, Mary

Mary, Mary, quite contrary
How does your garden grow?
With silver bells and cockle shells,
And pretty maids all in a row?

England, 1400s

❧

Monday's Child

Monday's child is fair of face,
Tuesday's child is full of grace.
Wednesday's child is full of woe.
Thursday's child has far to go.
Friday's child is loving and giving.
Saturday's child works hard for a living.
And the child who's born
on the Sabbath day
Is happy and healthy and loves always.

England, 1838

❧

Moon Song

I see the moon and the moon sees me.
The moon sees somebody I'd like to see.
God bless the moon and God bless me
And God bless somebody, I'd like to see.

England between 1500–1800 — Origin uncertain (many variations)

❧

John Wilson

My Little Pig

I had a little pig. I fed him in a trough.
He got so fat, his tail popped off!

Unable to find the origin

࿒࿒

My Little Rooster

I had a little rooster and fed him on dough.
He got so fat, he couldn't crow!

Unable to find the origin

࿒࿒

My Nose Itches

My nose itches.
I smell peaches.
Yonder comes a man with a hole in his britches.

Unable to find origin

࿒࿒

Nighttime Prayer

Now I lay me down to sleep.
I pray the Lord my soul to keep.
If I should die before I wake,
I pray the Lord my soul to take.

Unable to find the origin

࿒࿒

Old King Cole

Old King Cole was a merry old soul.
A merry old soul was he.
He called for his pipe and he called for his drums
And he called for his fiddlers – three.

England—Around 1700

࿒࿒

Old Mother Hubbard

Old Mother Hubbard
went to her cupboard
to get her poor doggie a bone.
But when she got there, the cupboard was bear,
and so the poor doggie had none.

England—Late 1700s

Old Tom Tackum

Old Tom Tackum met Bum Backum on his way to
Whirley Whickey Whackum.
Said Tom Tackum to Old Bum Backum, come and go with me to
Whirly Whickey Whackum.

Unable to find origin

One, Two, Buckle My Shoe

One, two, buckle my shoe.
Three, four, shut the door.
Five, six, pick up sticks.
Seven, eight, shut the gate.
Nine, ten, a big fat hen.

England—Sometime after 1600

Georgey Porgey

Georgey Porgey, Puddin' and Pie,
Kissed the girls and made them cry!
All the little boys and girls came
out to play.
Georgey Porgey ran away!

(Also heard as Orgey Porgey)
England—Unable to find time origin

Nancy Conatser, Marshes Siding, KY

Patty Cake

Patty cake, patty cake,
A baker's man.
Make me a cake as fast as you can.
Roll it and pat it and mark it with "B"
Then throw it in the oven for baby and me.
Patty cake, patty cake,
A baker's man.
Roll it up, roll it up, and throw it in the pan!

England, 1698

Peas Porridge

Pease porridge hot, peas porridge cold.
Some like it in the pot—nine days old.

Unable to find the origin

Peas Pudding

Peas pudding hot, peas pudding cold
Peas pudding in the pot, nine days old!
Some like it hot, some like it cold—
Peas pudding in the pot, nine days old.

Unable to find the origin

Penny

Find a penny, pick it up.
All the day you'll have good luck.
Find a penny, let it lay.
Bad luck will follow you all the day.

Unable to find the origin

Peter, Peter

Peter, Peter, pumpkin eater,
Had a wife and couldn't keep her.
So he put her in a pumpkin shell
And there he kept her very well!

England, 1600s

∾

Purple Cow

I never saw a purple cow.
I never hope to see one.
But let me tell you one thing!
I'd rather see than be one!

United States, 1895

∾

Pussy Cat, Pussy Cat

Pussy cat, pussy cat, where have you been?
I've been to London to visit the queen.
Pussy cat, pussy cat, what did you there?
I frightened a little mouse under her chair!

England, 1805

∾

Puss Is in the Well

Ding, dong bell! Puss is in the well!
Who put her in?
Little Johnny Flynn
Who'll pull her out?
Little Johnny Stout.

England, 1623

∾

Rain

Rain, rain, go away!
Come again another day.
Little Sally wants to play.

England, 1500s

❧

Ring Around the Rosies

Ring around the rosies, a pocket full of posies.
Ashes to ashes, we all fall down!

England, 1881

❧

Rock-a-Bye Baby

Rock-a-bye baby in the tree top.
When the wind blows, the cradle will rock.
When the bough breaks, the cradle will fall.
And down will come baby — cradle and all.

England, 1700s

❧

Roses Are Red

Roses are red.
Violets are blue.
Angels in heaven,
Know I love you.

England, 1784

❧

Rover

I had an old dog and his name was Rover.
He lay right down and died all over.

America, 1800s

❧

Simple Simon

Simple Simon met a pie man going to the fair.
Said Simple Simon to the pie man,
"Let me taste your ware."
Then said the pie man to simple Simon,
"I do not think it fair,
For you who have no money to want to taste my ware."

England, 1600s

❦

St. Ives

I met a man on his way to St. Ives.
This old man had seven wives.
These old women had seven sons
And every one was a son of a gun!

England, 1764

❦

Tea Pot

I'm a little teapot, strong and stout.
Here is my handle. Here is my spout.
Just tip me over and pour me out.

America, 1939

❦

The Crooked Man

I met a crooked man with a crooked little smile.
He used a crooked stick and he walked a crooked mile.
He had a crooked cat that chased a crooked mouse
and they all lived together in a crooked little house.

England, 1842

❦

The Itsy Bitsy Spider

The itsy bitsy spider climbed up the water spout.
Down came the rain and washed the spider out.
Out came the sun and dried up all the rain
And the itsy bitsy spider climbed up the spout again.

USA Around 1900

∽o∾

The Little Piggies

This little piggy went to market.
This little piggy went to town.
This little piggy had roast beef.
This little piggy had none.
And this little piggy cried,
"Wee, wee, wee," all the way home!

Unable to find the origin

∽o∾

The Mulberry Bush

Round and round the mulberry bush, the monkey chased the weasel.
The monkey stopped to pull up his socks and,
"Pop!" goes the weasel.

England, 1840s

∽o∾

Three Blind Mice

Three blind mice, three blind mice.
See how they run, see how they run.
They all chased after the farmer's wife,
Who cut off their tails with a carving knife.
Did you ever see such a sight in your life
As three blind mice!

England, 1805

∽o∾

Three Little Kittens

Three little kittens, they've lost their mittens, So they began to cry.
"Oh mother dear, see here, see here! Our mittens we have lost."
"What? Lost your mittens? You naughty kittens!
Then you shall have no pie!"
Then the three little kittens, they found their mittens
and they began to sigh.
"Oh mother dear, see here, see here! Our mittens we have found."
"You've found your mittens? You darling kittens!
Then you shall have some pie!"

USA, 1853

∽ი∾

The Old Woman Who Lived in a Shoe

There was an old woman who lived in a shoe.
She had so many younguns; she didn't know what to do!
She gave them some broth without any bread,
then whipped them all soundly and put them to bed!

England, 1794

∽ი∾

The Wise Old Owl

A wise old owl lived in an oak.
The more he saw, the less he spoke.
The less he spoke, the more he heard.
That old owl was a wise old bird!

USA — Origin Unknown

∽ი∾

The Wishing Star

Star light, star bright, the first star I see tonight . . .
I wish I may, I wish I might have the wish I wish tonight.

USA, Late 19th century

∽ი∾

Twinkle, Twinkle Little Star

Twinkle, twinkle little star. How I wonder what you are.
Up above the world so high, like a diamond in the sky.
I wish I may, I wish I might, have the wish I with tonight!

England, 1806

～○～

What Are Children Made Of?

Little girls are made of sugar and spice
and everything nice.
Little boys are made of snakes and snails
and puppy dog tails.

England, 1820

～○～

Wiglum Waglum

As I went to Wiglum Waglum,
There I found old Tom Tiglum Taglum.
I called old Hellum Bellum
To chase Tom Tiglum Taglum
Out of Wiglum Waglum.

Unable to find the origin

～○～

*J.W. Creech standing
in front of logs —
Putney, KY*

~ *Riddles* ~

Front Row: Sarah Jane, Isaiah, and Matilda Belcher
Middle Row: Cynthia and Polly Belcher, James Saylor
Back Row: Elhannon and Lucy Saylor Collins, Jack Bailey (uniform),
Milt Caldwell, and Eli Wilson

Riddles were an ancient form of entertainment throughout Europe and around the world for many centuries and continue today as a form of mind challenging verbal puzzles.

Origins to these riddles were not discovered by this author. They may have been created in Europe and brought to America through oral traditions, or may have been made up in mountain communities simply for the pleasure of a good riddle.

All Over the Fields

What goes all over the fields
And comes and sits
In your refrigerator at night?

(milk)

✎⟀☙

Around the World

It goes around the world
And comes around
To lock your windows at night.

(moon)

✎⟀☙

Blackie

Blackie goes in Blackie.
Blackie comes out Blackie
And leaves Whitey in Blackie.

(A black hen goes in a black stump and lays a white egg.)

✎⟀☙

Body with No Head

What has a body and no head,
Arms and no hands,
Legs and no feet?

(a pair of long handle underwear)

✎⟀☙

Hod Tody

Hod Tody,
Two heads and one body.

(barrel)

✎⟀☙

Sam and Sim Blevins, 1910

Head and Foot

What has a head but can't talk,
A foot, but can't walk?

(a bed)

⋙०⋘

Red and White

What's red and white and green all over
with little black men inside?

(watermelon)

⋙०⋘

Round as a Biscuit

I'm as round as a biscuit and busy as a bee?
The prettiest little thing that you ever did see!
What am I?

(watch)

⋙०⋘

Four Down Hangers

What has two hookers,
Two lookers,
Four down hangers,
And a switch about?

(a cow)

⋙०⋘

Whizzy Busy

Whizzy busy on the wall.
If you touch whizzy busy,
whizzy busy will bite you all!

(hornets' nest)

⋙०⋘

Riddlum Roddy

Riddlum, riddlum, riddlum, roddy?
What has a head, and yet no body?

(*a tadpole*)

≫∘≪

St. Ives

As I was going to old St. Ives,
I met a man with seven wives.
The seven wives had seven sacks.
Each sack had seven cats.
Each cat had seven kits.
Kits, cats, sacks, and wives.
How many were on their way to St. Ives?

(*one — I was going to St. Ives*)

≫∘≪

Love I Stand

Love I set,
Love I stand.
Love I hold in my right hand.
Love I see in yonder tree.

(*It is said that a man had been unjustly accused of a crime for which he would
be hanged. If he could create a riddle that the judge [or king] couldn't figure
out, he would be set free. He killed his dog, whose name was Love. He put a
piece of the dog in his back pocket, a piece in his shoe, a piece in the tree. He
was released because no one could figure out the riddle.*)

≫∘≪

Crooked as a Rainbow

Crooked as a rainbow,
teeth like a cat . . .
guess all night and you'll not guess what!

(*briar*)

≫∘≪

High as a House

High as a house,
Low as a mouse,
Bitter as gall,
Sweet after all.

(walnut)

∽ი∾

Can't Climb Up

Can't climb up.
Can't climb down.
There it goes,
Around and around.

(chimney smoke)

∽ი∾

House Full

A house full,
A yard full,
And can't catch a spoon full.

(smoke)

∽ი∾

Hot to the Touch

Hot to the touch
Warm to the nose,
The longer he stands
The shorter he grows.

(a candle)

∽ი∾

High as a House

High as a house,
Low as a mouse,
Has as many rooms as any man's house.

(honeycomb)

∾o∾

Black, White, and Read

What is black and white and read all over?

(a newspaper; the Bible)

∾o∾

The Peeper

What surrounds your house all the day
and peeps in at every window?

(sunshine)

∾o∾

Trackless

What circles around and around your house
And never leaves a track?

(the wind)

∾o∾

*Sarah, Irene, and Doug Boggs
Roark's Branch, KY*

Green as Grass

Green as grass and grass it ain't.
White as milk and milk it ain't.
Red as blood and blood it ain't.
Black as ink and ink it ain't.
(blackberry—from briar to bud,

to unripened berry, to fruit)

✧

The Singer

What sings, yet has no voice?

(a tea kettle)

✧

Hold It

You can only hold it for a minute
But it has no weight at all.

(your breath)

✧

Eat Your Home

I'll eat your home
And I'll eat your bones.
And I'll be sweeter for it.

(honey comb)

✧

Big at the Bottom

What's big at the bottom,
little at the top,
and a thing in the middle that goes flippity flop?

(a churn)

✧

Can't Fill it Up

What's round as a saucer,
But deeper than a cup
and the whole Cumberland River
Couldn't fill it up?

(a sieve)

～○～

Give

The more you give the more you have.
The more you have the more you give.

(love)

～○～

London Bridge

As I crossed over London bridge,
I met a very fine man.
He tipped his hat and drew his cane.
Can you tell me now, his name?

(Andrew)

～○～

Round as a Ball

Round as a ball,
Sharp as an awl,
And way up in the air.

(chestnut burr)

～○～

Up

What goes everywhere but up?

(water)

～○～

The Follower

What follows you around
all day unless it rains —
then it runs away?

(*your shadow*)

Molly and Berry Napier
Grays Knob, KY

Round as a Tree

What is round as a tree,
And deep as a cup,
But all the king's men
Can't pull it up?

(*a well*)

The Weeper

What weeps, but never cries?

(*the willow tree*)

Two Backbones

What has two backbones and
Ten thousand ribs?

(*railroad track*)

A Hill Full

A hill full;
a hole full;
but you can't get a bowl full.

(*fog*)

125

Eyes

What has eyes but cannot see?

(a potato)

Ears

What has ears but cannot hear?

(corn)

Chimney

What goes up the chimney down
and can't go down the chimney up?

(umbrella)

Four Legs

What walks on four legs when it's young,
two legs when it's grown,
and three legs at the end when it's almost gone?

*(a man: He crawls on all fours as a baby, walks on two legs as a man,
and must use a cane in his old age.)*

King

A king met a king in a long lane.
To the king said the king, "What is your name?"
Silver is my saddle, brass is my bow.
I've told you my name, three times in a row.

(King)

Two Backbones

What has two backbones and
Ten thousand ribs?

(a railroad track)

❦

Shucked and Plucked

The old man shucked it and plucked it.
The old woman raised her dress and caught it.
What was it?

(The old man shook apples from the tree. The old woman used her skirt tail as an apron to catch them.)

❦

What Has?

What has a head, but has no hair?

(a pin)

❦

What has lots of holes, but still holds water?

(a sponge)

❦

What has a head, but cannot think?

(a match)

❦

What has a tongue, but cannot speak?

(a shoe)

❦

What has teeth, but can't eat?

(a comb)

❦

What has legs, but can't walk?

(a table; a chair)

❦

127

What has the ability to run, but can't walk?

(a nose; a river)

What has gold, but it can't buy?

(an egg yolk)

What has a path up and down, but can't touch the ground?

(a pump handle)

What has a ring, but no fingers?

(a cow bell)

What has a great big head and no body?

(a tadpole)

What has an eye but can't see?

(a needle)

What has many eyes but can't see?

(a lace up shoe or boot)

What has two hands but no fingers?

(a clock)

Eyes that Can't See

What has eyes that can't see,
A tongue that can't talk,
And a soul that can't be saved?

(a shoe)

Sunday Dinner on the Ground
Pine Mountain, KY

Box suppers, socials, frolics, quilting bees, barn raisings, chivarees, revivals, singings, funerals, hay rides, and harvest time all provided opportunities for mountain folk to come together for times of community, family, and fellowship. One of the favorite gatherings was for a homecoming event, often accompanied by "Dinner on the Ground" or a kind of potluck where everyone brought food and all were welcome to share in the bounty.

Superstitions

*Marie Hamlin, Harvey Wilson, Gracie Hamlin
(Note the handkerchief between Harvey and
Gracie, who were dating at the time of the
photo and not allowed to hold hands.)*

Superstitions have been observed through the ages. Some came out of actual experiences while others were born from fears or hopes. Appalachia is rich with superstitions handed down from one generation to the next.

Jami Burkhart and
Rhonda Long Robinson

A

accident

- Never laugh at someone who has an accident. If you do, the same thing will happen to you.

- If an accident has put a person in a wheelchair, you must never sit in that wheelchair or the same accident will happen to you.

- Never walk on someone else's crutches to see how they feel or you will need them for real!

- If you wish an accident on someone, it will come to you instead, or to one you love.

acorn

- Carry an acorn in your pocket for good luck.

- Sew an acorn into the hem of a quilt that you will sleep under for good luck.

- Keep an acorn on the mantle for good luck.

- Place an acorn over the facing of the entrance door to protect from evil passing through the door.

anointing oil

- Place anointing oil in the door post and lentils of every room in the house to insure peace.

- Place anointing oil on the head of each bed in the house to insure sweet dreams.

- Place anointing oil under the regular seat or under the bed of an unruly child to improve their behavior.

angels

- If you see an angel, you will be blessed.

- If someone gives you an angel doll that doesn't have eyes on the face, do not embroider eyes onto the doll or sew buttons on for eyes. If you do, the doll will steal your soul.

apples

- An apple a day keeps the doctor away.
- If you can peel the skin from an apple completely without breaking it, the peel will form the first letter of the person's name you are going to marry.
- If you have an apple with a stem, think of potential sweethearts' names. With each twist of the stem, name one of them. The name that corresponds to the twist that breaks the stem is the one you should seek out.
- If you can peel an apple skin completely without breaking it, you will have good luck.
- If you can break an apple in two using only your hands, you will have your love returned by whomever you choose.

arms

- If you have hairy arms, you will be very wealthy.

arrowhead

- If you find an arrowhead it will bring you good luck if you put it away and save it.
- If you find an arrowhead and toss it away, it will bring you bad luck.

ashes

- Don't take any ashes out of your house between Christmas and New Years Day or you'll have bad luck.

B

baby

- It is bad luck to put a baby's clothes on over its head before it is one year old.
- Pull the baby's clothes on over it's feet instead of over its head until it is one year old, or it will never grow.
- When a new baby is born into a family, someone in that family will die.

Earl and Flonnie Bryant
McCreary County, KY

133

- To determine the sex of a baby, stick a threaded sewing needle in the end of a pencil and suspend it over the pregnant woman's wrist. If the pencil swings back and forth, the baby will be a boy. If it swings in a circle, it will be a girl.

- To determine the sex of an unborn baby, suspend the woman's wedding band by a string over her wrist. If it swings back and forth, the baby will be a boy. If it swings in a circle, the baby will be a girl.

- A blue eyed baby will be a happy child.
  A brown eyed baby will be gentle and mild.
  A green eyed baby will have envy and strife.
  A grey eyed baby will wander through life.

- The giver of the third gift to be opened at a baby shower will be the next one to be expecting a baby of their own!

bad

- If something bad has happened to you, walk backwards into your house when you arrive home. Before you start to leave the house again, you must sit on the floor and count to ten. This will make the bad luck go away.

- If you have had a lot of bad luck and nothing seems to work to make it go away, the last thing to try is to spit over your little finger. But make sure you have tried everything else first, because that is the last thing you can do to make bad luck go away.

bald men

- To make fun of a bald man is bad luck. In the Bible, when a group of children made fun of the prophet Elijah for being bald headed, he called down a bear from the mountains and it devoured them.

- Rubbing a bald headed man's scalp will bring you good luck.

- Bald headed men make better sweethearts.

bandages

- Never save someone else's bandage to be used again. It will certainly bring bad luck.

Annie and Enos Hensley — Smith, KY

Sim Blevins   *Opal Blevins*

- Never wear someone else's bandage. You will have need of it again if you do.
- Only the person whom a bandage belongs to should ever use it for anything.

baseball

- Spit on a new baseball bat and hit it on the ground three times before you bat with it. This will bring good luck.
- Spit into your hand before picking up the bat when it is your turn to bat to bring good luck.
- If you hit a homerun with a specific bat, always use that bat again when you go up to bat.
- If you strike out using a particular bat, do not use that bat again!
- Get the best baseball player you know to spit on your new glove before you use it and you will have good luck every time you use that mitt.
- Spit in your mitt before a game to bring good luck.

basketball

- Don't dribble a basketball in the house or it will bring bad luck.
- Spit on your hand and rub it on the bottom of your shoe before a game to bring good luck.
- Wear the same underwear you wore when you won the last game if you want to insure a winning streak.

Polly Asher

- Never change to a different pair of shoes once the season has started.
- Wear the same socks after winning a game at the next game – without washing.

bed

- If you leave a hat lying on the bed, it will bring bad luck.
- If you get out of bed on the left side in the morning, it will bring bad luck.
- If you lay a wet umbrella on a bed, the person who usually sleeps there will get sick.
- If you set your bed in the middle of the room, it is very bad luck. That is why most people place their beds in the corner of the room.
- Make sure you get out of bed on the same side that you went to bed the night before or you will have bad luck.
- Never put your shoes on the bed. It will bring bad luck to whoever sleeps there. They will travel all night in their dreams and not rest.
- Once you start to make up a bed, do not let anything interrupt you until you are finished or the person who sleeps there will be restless.
- If you can't make a bed well, you will marry a worthless man.
- If you get up out of bed on the opposite side of what you got into bed the night before, you will be grouchy all day long.

bees

- If a man keeps bees, when he dies, the bees will either leave the hive or they will die.
- If a bee gets in your house, it is a sign of company coming.
- If a swarm of bees gathers on a rooftop, it is a sign that the house will burn down.
- If bees swarm in May, there will plenty of hay.
- If the beekeeper dies, someone must go to his beehives and tell them of his death. If not, the bees will leave when he doesn't return to visit the hives.

- If a beekeeper dies, someone must go to the bees and tell them, "I am your new master. You belong to me now," or they will swarm and go somewhere else.

bell

- Every time a bell rings, an angel gets its wings.
- If you hear bells ringing in your ears, they are death bells. Someone you love is going to die.
- If you hear the tinkle of bells in an unlikely place, where there are no bells, a soul is passing by, a fairy, or an angel.
- If you hear bells or chimes when there are none to be found, a spirit is saying hello.

birds

- If a black bird gets in your house, it is a sign of bad luck.
- If a black bird dies in your house, someone is going to die.
- If a black bird pecks at your window, someone in your house is going to die.
- If a bird beats its wings against the window, you are going to hear bad news.
- If the first robin you see in springtime is flying upward, you will have good luck.
- If the first robin you see in springtime is flying down to the ground, you will have bad luck.
- If a whip-oor-will lands on your house, it is a sign that someone is going to die.
- If a rooster crows in the middle of the night, it is a sign of death.
- If you see a red bird flying, it's a sign of company coming.
- If you have a red bird come and sit on your house, it is a sign of company coming to stay for a while.

Carty Asher

137

- If you see two redbirds together in the same place, make a wish. They will bring you good luck.
- If a bird flies into a closed window of your house, it is a sign of bad luck.
- If a bird lands on the path in front of you, you will have good luck.
- It is good luck to see a falcon.
- It is bad luck to hear a hen crow. You must kill her right away.
- If a dove lands on your window ceil, it is bringing you good luck.
- If you see a red bird, watch it until it flies out of sight without taking your eyes off of it and without blinking. Make a wish and it will come true. Luck.
- If you catch a humming bird and let it go, it will grant you one wish.
- If you kill a humming bird, it is bad luck.
- If you see a redbird and blow it a kiss, it will carry the kiss to your sweetheart.
- If you see two cardinals together, make a wish. It is very good luck.
- If you put salt on a bird's tail, you can catch it.

birth
- The day a child is born on is important to that child's future:
    Monday's child is fair of face;
    Tuesday's child is full of grace;
    Wednesday's child is full of woe;
    Thursday's child has far to go;
    Friday's child is loving and giving;
    Saturday's child will work hard for a living;
    But the child that is born on the Sabbath Day is fair and wise, good and gay. (gay = good)
- A knife under the bed of a woman giving birth will cut the pain.
- Tie a red ribbon around the mother's wrist during delivery to bind her to this world.
- If a pregnant woman craves a food she doesn't get while she is with child, the baby will have a birth mark shaped like that food.

blowing

- If you can blow all the seeds off of a dead dandelion in one breath, you can make a wish and it will come true.

- If you blow out all the candles on your birthday cake, you can make a wish and it will come true.

Sampson Curry, Jr., Delbert Wayne, and Mary Eva Vance Curry

blue

- Wearing blue will protect you from witches.
- A bride should wear something blue on her wedding day.
- If you wear blue all the time, you will die early.
- A blue door will protect you against witches.

borrowing

- If you borrow something in another person's container, the container must not be returned to them empty.

brag

- If you brag about something, make sure you knock on wood nine times, or the thing you bragged about will disappear.
- If you brag on a thing, it will be taken from you.

bread

- If your cornbread is rough, your husband's face will be rough.
- If you scorch your cornbread, your husband will come home angry that day.
- If you won't share your bread, your dough won't rise.
- If your cornbread burns, you have an angry husband.
- A girl who can't make bread will never be wed.

bridal showers

- If the bride breaks a ribbon, that represents one child she will have in her marriage. (three broken ribbons — three children, etc.)

- The giver of the third gift that is opened will have a baby next.
- Every time the future bride says the groom's name during her bridal shower, is a predictor of how many years that the bride and groom will be together.
- Gather all of the ribbons and bows from the bridal shower and collect them into a bouquet for the wedding rehearsal. It is good luck for the woman walking in the bride's place at rehearsal to carry them.

briars

- If you get tangled in a briar and can get yourself free without ripping your clothes, you will have good luck.
- If you clear your land of briars and thorns and burn them and they all turn into ashes, your land will be blessed. If they refuse to burn, you will have trouble on that land as long as you live there.

bride (see also **wedding**)

- A bride must carry: Something old, something new, something borrowed, something blue.
- A bride must marry in white if she expects her life to go right.
- If a bride sees a rainbow on her wedding day, her marriage will always be blessed.
- If a bride sees an open grave on her wedding day, it is an omen of very bad luck.

Mancie and Mary Shelley—McCreary Co., Kentucky

- It is good luck to have a bride wear anything of yours on her wedding day.
- If a bride walks through a spider web by accident, it is good luck.
- Happy the bride whom the sun shines on. Tears for the bride that the rain falls on.
- It is good luck to carry another bride's handkerchief on your wedding day.
- It is good luck for a bride to carry a penny in her shoe.

bridge

- Do not say good-bye to someone while standing on a bridge. Your relationship will end.
- If you say good-bye to someone on a bridge, you will never see them again.
- Do not kiss on a bridge. Your love may run out.

broom

- If you sweep under someone's feet while they are sitting down, they will never marry.
- Never move into a new house and take the broom with you from the old house. If you do, all the troubles from the old house will follow you into the new.
- If you move to a new house, you must get a new broom. Make sure you carry something else into the house before you carry in the broom.
- It is good luck for a bride and groom to jump over a broom stick.
- If someone is sweeping with a broom and they accidentally hit you with that broom, you will have bad luck.
- Sweep with a broom (or run a vacuum) on Sunday and all week long you'll have bad luck.
- If a broom has fallen over on the floor and you step over the handle instead of picking it up, you will never be a good housekeeper.
- If you want to know if someone is a witch or not, lay a broomstick across the door and ask them to come inside. If they are a witch, they will not come across the broom stick.
- Never step over a broom. It will surely bring bad luck.
- Never carry a broken broom all the way through the house. Take it out the back door and get rid of it, or you will have bad luck.
- To break a broom is bad luck.
- It is bad luck to chase someone with a broom.
- When you are sweeping the floor with a straw broom, watch for straws that come out of the broom. If you see one when it comes out, pick it up, name it, and place the straw over the door. The person you have named will come through that door.

- If a broom handle falls across the door, bad luck will come to the next person who crosses the floor unless they pick up the broom and restore it to its former position.

buckeye

- Carry a buckeye in your pocket for good luck.
- Sew a buckeye into the corner of a new quilt and the people who sleep under it will have good luck.

butterfly

- If a butterfly lands on you, you will have good luck.
- If a butterfly lands on your dress, you will get a new dress (blouse, coat, pants, shoes, etc.)
- If the first butterfly you see in spring is white, you will have good luck that summer.
- If the first butterfly you see in spring is white, you will soon be invited to a wedding.
- If the first butterfly you see in spring is white and you are a single woman, it means you will marry soon.
- If the first butterfly you see in spring is black, you will have back luck that summer.
- If you see three butterflies together, you will have good luck.

button

- If you find a two eyed button it is good luck.

C

candle

- If someone you love is traveling, light a candle in the window until they get home to guide them on their way.

car

- If you wash your car, it is sure to rain.
- Whoever drives to begin a trip must be the one driving when the trip ends.

cards

- If you are playing cards and you drop one on the floor, whatever suit it is will come to your door.

  If you drop a HEART, love will come to your door.

  If you drop a SPADE, bad luck will come to your door.

  If you drop a DIAMOND, money will come to your door.

  If you drop a CLUB, good luck will come to your door.

cats

- If a black cat crosses your path, it is bad luck. To remove the bad luck, you have to spit on the path before you continue on.

- If your cat eats a snail, that will bring bad luck for sure.

- Never let a group of cats surround you on all sides. If you do, they will mark you for bad luck.

- It is lucky to own a solid gray cat.

- If you let a black cat walk beside of you without trying to shoo it away or be mean to it, it will bring you no bad luck and may even bring you good luck.

- If a cat sneezes directly on you, it is bringing you good luck.

- Never try to catch a wild or stray cat and make it stay with you. If you force it to stay, it will only bring bad luck. If, however, you let the cat make up its own mind about staying, you will have good luck.

- When no one is looking, cats can turn into other stuff. They can also blend into other stuff so that they appear invisible, and they can climb walls if they want to.

- If you dress a cat up, you will have bad luck.

- If a strange cat follows you all the way home, it is bringing good luck to your doorstep.

- If a gray cat paces back and forth in front of you, you will have good luck for sure.

- Never chase a black cat. Bad luck will chase you.

Lewis Stephens Family
McCreary County, KY

- If you see three black cats on Halloween day, it is a bad sign for sure.
- If a black cat crosses your path, cross your arms in front of you and leave them that way until the cat has gone.
- If a black cat comes and sits in front of you, make the sign of an "X" across your chest to break the bad luck.
- When you are driving, if a black cat crosses in front of you, make an "X" on the windshield with your pointer finger before you proceed.
- If a black cat crosses in front of you, you must find a loose thread in your clothing and pull it out to break the bad luck.
- You will always have good luck if you can make friends with stray cats.
- A cat washing its face in front of the door is a sign of company coming.
- A cat in a coal mine is bad luck.
- If a gray cat crosses your path, it is a sign of very good luck coming your way.
- If a white cat crosses your path, it is a sign of good luck to come.
- If you want to keep a stray cat, let it see itself in the mirror and it will never leave you.
- If you want to keep a stray cat, butter its paw and it will never leave you.
- If a white cat suddenly appears in your house, then vanishes, it is a sign that someone in your family is going to die very soon and unexpectedly.
- If a cat walks back and forth in front of you two times and you don't chase it away, bad luck will come to you.
- Never treat a cat cruelly. As surely as you do, bad luck will find you.
- If you step on a cat's tail, it will bring you bad luck.
- Do not keep a cat in the house with a newborn baby. The cat will stand on the baby's chest and suck the oxygen out of its lungs and kill it.
- It is very bad luck to drown a cat.
- It is bad luck to own a solid grey cat or a solid black cat.

- If a cat follows you all the way home from a distance, do not run it off. It is bringing good luck to your home if you let it stay.
- Never let a group of cats surround you on all sides. They are gathering to bring very bad luck to you.
- If your cat sits in front of your door washing its face with its paws, someone you know is going to come and see you. If a strange cat sits in front of your door and washes its face with its paws, a stranger is coming to see you.
- If you take a black cat and rub its fur in the dark, sparks will fly out of the fur.

cedar trees

- If you plant a cedar tree, when it gets big enough to cover your grave, you will die.
- Don't plant a cedar tree. It will invite death into your family.

cemetery

- Hold your breath when you drive past a cemetery. If you don't, you may breathe in a spirit of someone recently deceased.

chalk

- If you accidentally get chalk dust in your eyes, you won't be going to school the next day.
- If you drop a piece of chalk and it shatters, bad luck is coming your way.
- If you drop a piece of chalk and it stays solid in one piece, good luck is coming your way.

cheeks

- If your cheeks burn, your sweetheart is talking about you.

cherry

- If you can tie a cherry stem into a knot inside your mouth, using your tongue and teeth only, you can be assured that the person you love will fall deeply in love with you.

children

- The number of wrinkles in your forehead represents the number of children you will have.

- When a bride and groom are opening wedding presents, they will have the number of children according to the number of ribbons they break while unwrapping the presents.

- The number of lines in your palm that form an "X" show how many children you will have.

- Take all the seeds from one bite of watermelon. You must eat the watermelon and spit the seeds in your hand. Then open your hand and smack the seeds against your forehead. If any stick, count the number of seeds and that is how many children you will have. White seeds are for girls. Black seeds are for boys.

chill

- If you get a sudden chill for no apparent reason, it means a ghost is in the room with you.

- If you get a sudden shiver of cold, someone has walked over your grave (where you will be buried in the future).

- If you get an unexplained chill, a rabbit just ran over your grave.

- If you get gooseflesh for no apparent reason, a goose just walked over the place where you will be buried.

*Matt, Charlie, and
Bud Stephens*

Christmas

- On the real Christmas Eve, at midnight, the animals can speak in human voices for one hour. (Some say this is 10 days after the Christmas celebrated on the current calendar; some say 12.

- On the real Christmas Eve, at midnight, all the animals bow down on their knees to worship the Lord.

- Don't take any ashes out of your house between Christmas and New Year's Day or you will have bad luck.

- If you bring smooth holly into your house at Christmas, the wife will rule the household that year. If you bring prickly holly into the house for Christmas, the husband will rule the household that year.
- Spread rosemary greens in front of the door at Christmas. Whoever walks on them will be blessed.
- A candle in the window on Christmas Eve is to welcome people to your home and will bring you good luck.
- If you light a candle on Christmas day and it goes and it goes out before sunset, you will have bad luck in the coming year. If it burns until after sunset, your luck for the year will be good.
- If a child is bad during the year, Santa will leave a bundle of switches in their stocking or a lump of coal.
- If you see the Christmas star and make a wish, it will come true.
- A star at the top of the Christmas tree is because the Wise Men followed the star on the first Christmas. A star on top of the tree will bring all of your family safely home for the holiday.
- Put a sprig of holly on your beehives at Christmas and they will make a lot of delicious honey that year.
- Holly in the house at Christmas will bring good luck and happiness all through the holiday season.
- If you stand under the mistletoe, you will get kissed.
- If you put mistletoe over a door, it is bad luck to take it down unless someone has been kissed beneath
- If a single girl lives in the house, you should put mistletoe over the door. If she doesn't get kissed under it, she won't be getting married that year.
- If a married couple kisses under the mistletoe, they will have a happy marriage.

circles

- If you find a circle or ring of mushrooms growing wild, it is called a fairy ring or a wishing ring. Stand inside the circle and make a wish, but you cannot tell where the circle is or what your wish was or it won't come true.

- If you stand in a circle, a witch can't harm you.
- If you make a circle of salt around yourself, no evil can come to you in that circle.
- Make a circle of salt around your bed and no harm will come to you while you sleep.

clocks

- If you have a clock that hasn't been working and it suddenly chimes, it marks the death of someone in your family.
- If someone dies in a room with a clock, you must stop the clock at the time of that person's death.

coins

- If you throw a coin in the river and leave it there, it will bring you good luck.
- If you spit on a coin and make a wish, then throw it behind you and never look back, and if an elf or a Leprechaun finds it, they will make sure your wish comes true.
- If you place a coin where an elf or a Leprechaun can find it, they will bring you good luck.
- If you find a penny or any other coin on heads, pick it up and save it. It will bring you good luck.
- If you find a coin and spend it, you will have no good luck.
- If you find a coin on tails, leave it laying or bad luck will claim you.

corn

- If you go to a corn shucking, the first man to find a red ear of corn is lucky. He will get to kiss the prettiest girl there.
- If a woman finds the first red ear of corn in a corn shucking, she gets to pick her partner to dance with later, or if the group didn't believe in dancing, she could pick the man she wanted to walk her home.

cowlick

- A cowlick means you're made of strong stuff.

- If your cowlick sticks up, it means you're about to be in a temper. (bad mood; angry)

crack

- If you step on a crack, you will break your mother's back.

cricket

- If a cricket gets in your house, it brings good luck.
- NEVER kill a cricket that gets in your house or all of your luck will turn bad.
- A cricket in the house will warn you of bad weather.

cross

- Always wear a cross to keep away evil spirits.
- If a black cat walks in front of you, cross your arms across your chest until the cat has gone out of sight to ward off bad luck.

crows

- Don't count crows.
- If a black crow pecks on your window, someone will die in your house.

crutches

- NEVER ever walk on someone else's crutches. If you do, you will end up with an injury worse than theirs!

cry

- Every time you cry, for every teardrop, a flower will die.
- For every tear you shed a flower will bloom somewhere.

cutting teeth

- When a baby is born, take a pencil or a marker and write the child's name all over a raw unbroken eggshell. Put the eggshell away in a safe place where it won't get broken. Don't check on it; don't ever look at it again. When that baby cuts teeth, you won't even know it. The child will not cry or fret at all while teething.
- Let a baby chew on a piece of whittled cedar wood to help cut teeth.

D

dandelions

- If you carry dandelions in your pocket, you don't have to worry about werewolves.
- If you can blow all the seeds off of a dead dandelion in one breath, make a wish and it will come true.
- If you want to know how many children you will have, take a dead dandelion that has gone to seed and blow as hard as you can. However many seeds are left represent the number of children you will have.

death

- If someone dies and you go to the graveyard the night they are buried, you will see their ghost.
- Death comes in threes.

deer

- If you kill a deer, you will have good luck.
- If you see a deer in the fog, it is good luck.

dew

- On the first day of May, a person should rise, go outside and gather enough dew to wash their face in without speaking a word to anyone. This guarantees good luck until the next year.

dish/dishes

- If you dash your dishwater out the back door, it will bring you bad luck because there may be a fairy, an elf, or a Leprechaun standing nearby. If you throw the water out and it gets one of them wet, they will bring you bad luck.
- If you drop a dish rag, someone is coming unexpectedly.
- If you get your belly wet while you do dishes, you will marry a drunk.

dog

- Never kill a dog. If you do, bad luck will follow you all the days of your life.

- A dog with one brown eye and one blue is a good dog and will bring you luck.
- If you get dog bit, it won't heal as long as the dog lives.

dog days

- If you swim during dog days, your sores won't heal.
- If you scratch at bug bites or sores in dog days, they will get very infected.
- If you swim in dog days, you are sure to get an earache.

Lena Roark
Roark Branch, KY

doors

- If you enter a house through one door, make sure you leave through the same door or you will have bad luck.
- If you leave a house through a door different than the one you entered, you will have bad luck.
- If you leave anything hanging on a doorknob, it will bring bad luck.
- A blue door will keep witches out of your house.
- If you sleep with your closet door open, it will bring bad luck.

dreams (See section on Dream Interpretations)

- If you wear a dream catcher necklace while you sleep, bad dreams will not come to you. It only works if you truly believe it.
- Dream at night—devil's delight.
  Dream in the morning—heed the angels' warning.
- Never tell a dream before breakfast. If you do, it will come true.

dress

- If the hem of your dress gets turned up by accident, hold it, make a wish, kiss the hem of your dress, and then fold it back down.

drop

- If you drop a knife on the floor, it is a sign that company is coming.
- If you drop a dishrag on the floor, it is a sign that company is coming.

- If you drop a teaspoon on the floor while you are doing dishes, it means your sweetheart will be coming to see you soon.
- If you drop a bite of something you were getting ready to put in your mouth, it means that someone around you wanted that bite.

duck

- If you catch a green headed duck, you will have good luck.

E

ears

- If your ears burn, someone is talking about you.
- If your ear itches, someone is talking about you.
- If your ears turn red, someone is talking about you. If it is your right ear, a woman is talking about you. If it is your left ear, a man is talking about you.
- If your ear itches and you throw salt over your shoulder, the first person you see with a toothache has been talking about you.
- If your ear itches at school, get ready for a surprise test.
- If your right ear itches, someone is talking good about you.
- If your left ear itches, someone is talking bad about you.

egg

- If you break an egg and it has a double yolk, you will have good luck.

eyebrows

- If your eyebrows grow together into a unibrow, you will be very rich.

eyelash

- If an eyelash falls on your cheek and someone sees it, make a wish. If they can blow it away, your wish will come true.
- If an eyelash falls out and you see it on yourself, put the eyelash on the back of your hand, blow it away and make a wish. It will come true.

eyes

- If you get chalk dust in your eyes, there will be no school the next day.
- If you cross your eyes on purpose and someone slaps you, they will stay crossed forever.
- If your left eye itches, you're going to be made happy.
- If your right eye itches, you're going to be made sad.
- If you have a sty on your eye, stand in the forks of the road and say, "Sty, sty, go off my eye and catch the next person that comes by." The sty will go off your eye and on to the next person.
- If your eye itches, you will be pleased before the day is over.
- If your right eye itches and you scratch it, you will cry before the day is over.
- If your left eye itches, don't scratch it and you'll get good news.
- If you make fun of someone sigoogled, your spouse will be too!

F

falling

- If a baby doesn't fall out of bed, it will die young.
- If you can catch a falling leaf, you will have good luck.
- If you catch a falling leaf, a letter from your sweetheart will come in the mail.
- If you can catch falling leaves, you will be pretty and happy all of your life.
- If you dream of falling and don't wake up before you hit the ground, you will die.

feet/foot

- If the bottoms of your feet itch, you will soon be walking on new ground.
- If a man steps his feet in Clover Fork, he'll always be drawn back to Harlan. (also applies to rivers and streams of other places)

fight

- If your knuckles itch, you are going to get in a fight.
- If you know you are going to be in a fight, make sure you don't have any pickles on you or in your pocket. If you do, you will lose for sure, and maybe get knocked out.

fingers

- If you are telling a lie, keep your fingers crossed behind your back so the person you are talking to won't figure it out.
- Cross your fingers and make a wish for good luck.
- If you can make your first and fourth fingers touch at the back of your hand without any help, you will rule your house.

fingernails/toenails

- If you cut your fingernails or toenails on Sunday, the devil will be after you all week.
- If you put fingernail clippings in a glass of lemonade and give it to the one you love, if he drinks it, he'll love you forever. (unless he finds out what you did!)
- If you want to insure good luck, always trim your fingernails and toenails by the light of the full moon.
- It is bad luck to cut your nails on Friday.
- Cuttings from your nails should be burned or buried.
- White spots on the fingernails mean you've told a lie—one spot for each lie.

Sarah and Elmer Boggs   *Doug Boggs*
Roark Branch—Breathitt County, KY

- Bite a baby's fingernails the first year of its life instead of cutting or clipping them and the baby will never be a thief.

fire

- If you play in fire, you'll wet your pants.
- If you play in fire, you'll wet the bed.
- If you build a fire that won't burn, your love is untrue.
- If you build a fire that will burn, your love is true.
- If a person can build a good fire with ease, it is because they have Indian blood in them.
- If you can build a fire easily, the one you love will love you in return.
- If your true love can easily build a fire, they will make a good husband or wife.

fish/fishing

- Toss back your first fish of the day and you'll have good luck all day long.
- If you count the fish you've caught, you won't catch any more that day.
- Spit on your bait before you cast it in the water.
- Don't let a pregnant woman carry your rod or bait.
- If you catch a sucker fish while you are fishing, it will bring you good luck.
- If you catch a blue crayfish (crawdad), it will bring you good luck.
- If you catch a fish with a coin in its mouth, you will always have enough money for the things you need, as long as you keep the coin.

flowers

- A single rose means, "I love you."
- If you take the petal from a flower and name it for your sweetheart, then blow through it and make it pop, that means your sweetheart love you.
- If you won't share your flowers, your flowers won't grow.

- If you pull the petals off of a flower with many petals (a daisy is best) and alternate saying, "Loves me/loves me not," with each petal, the last petal will tell you if your sweetheart truly loves you.

forget

- If you are fixing to say something and you forget what it was, it means that what you were going to say is a lie.

fork

- If you drop a fork, it means a man is coming to visit.
- If you accidentally end up with two forks at your dinner plate and you are single, it means your true love is not far away (a man).
- If you are setting the table for company and two forks accidentally end up at a woman's place instead of a fork and a spoon, it means she will have two husbands in her life.
- If a single woman ends up with an extra fork at her plate by accident, it means she will be married soon.

four leaf clover

- If you find a four leaf clover, pick it, and save it, you will have good luck.
- If you find a four leaf clover, pick it, and then throw it away, you will have bad luck.
- If you find a four leaf clover, place it on your tongue and swallow the whole thing on the first try, you can make a wish and it will come true.
- Press a four leaf clover in your Bible and keep it there for good luck.
- If someone gives you a four leaf clover they have found, they care about you deeply.
- If you can find four leaf clovers easily, you are a lucky person.
- To press and keep a four leaf clover in a book continues to bring good luck to the owner of the book.

Fridays

- Wearing black on Fridays will bring you bad luck.
- Every Friday 13 is bad luck, especially if you don't believe in it.

frogs

- If you let a frog pee on you, you will get warts.
- If you kill a frog, it will bring you bad luck.
- If a frog gets in your house, it will bring good luck, as long as you don't kill it.

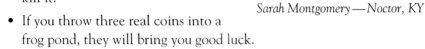

Joe Montgomery, Jane Bach, Sarah Montgomery—Noctor, KY

- If you throw three real coins into a frog pond, they will bring you good luck.
- If a toad frog moves in under your porch, he will bring you good luck as long as he lives peacefully there.
- If you kill a frog on purpose, your cow will give bloody milk.
- If you pull three hairs from your sweethearts head, comb, or brush and get a frog or toad to swallow them whole (wrapped around their food), then kiss the frog, your sweetheart is yours to keep.

funeral

- Do not count the cars in a funeral procession.
- A pregnant woman should not attend a funeral.
- Don't wear new shoes to a funeral.

G

garden

- If you pull something up out of the garden and the roots are short or broken off, you will have bad luck.
- Garter snakes in your garden will bring you good luck if you don't harm them. They will eat all of the bugs and keep them away.

garlic

- If you carry garlic in your clothes, or wear some in a pouch around your neck, it will keep evil away.
- Garlic will keep vampires away.

Jane Bach, Sarah Montgomery, Lena Roark — Noctor, KY

- If you place garlic salt in the four corners of your bedroom, you will not have bad dreams.
- If you place garlic salt at the four corners of your bed or between your mattresses, it will keep bad dreams away.

ghost

- A ghost will not cross water.
- If you call a deceased person's name three times while standing facing a mirror, you will see their face appear in the mirror.

grave

- If you walk backwards thirteen times around a grave, that person will speak to you.
- Count thirteen stars while you are lying in bed at night and then look under your bed. You'll see your coffin that you will be buried in.
- If flowers spring up on a new grave, that person lived a good life.
- If weeds spring up on a new grave, that person did not live a good life.

greens

- When you cook greens, you must cook them with a dime in the pot to bring good luck.
- When you serve greens that have been cooked with a dime in them, whoever is served up a helping that holds the dime will have good luck.

groom

- If the groom sees the bride on their wedding day before the ceremony, it brings very bad luck.
- If a groom misplaces the bride's wedding band, or loses it before the wedding, the wedding should not take place.
- If the groom drops the wedding band during the ceremony, the wedding is doomed.

- The groom should carry his bride over the threshold of their house the first time they enter to insure a happy marriage.

- The groom should send his bride a love letter on the eve of their wedding to bring abiding love.

H

hair

- If you take a red haired woman to be your wife, all your days you'll have trouble and strife.

- If you bury a hair from your head along with a hair from the head of the one you love together, you will one day be together.

- If you singe the ends of your hair on a new moon it will grow more quickly.

- If you wear a lock of your sweetheart's hair in your hat, he will love no other.

- If your hair stands up on your neck or the back of your head for no reason, someone is standing on your grave.

- If you can pull a hair from the head of someone you love without them knowing that you did, they will love you deeply.

- If you find a gray hair in your head, do not pull it out. If you do, two will grow back in its place.

- If you pull out a gray hair, ten will grow back in its place.

- If you take a piece of a person's hair and pull it through between the fingernails of the thumb and pointer finger, it will tell you if that person is jealous or not. If the hair curls, they are. If it doesn't curl, they are not.

- If you want your hair to grow fast, cut a lock of it and bury it under the leak of the house (eaves) where rain water will run over it.

- If you want to make your hair grow quickly, trim it and place it under the bottom step of the stairs so that everyone who uses those stairs to enter and leave the house will step on it.

- If you are the friend of the bride, sew a lock of your hair into the hem of her wedding dress. It will bring you a husband or good luck in your marriage if you are already married.
- If you burn your hair that lands in the floor after a haircut, you will have headaches.
- After a haircut, it is good luck to scatter the hair that was cut to the wind.
- If you are single and you find a hair in the heel of your stocking, it will be the color hair of the person you are going to marry.
- If a pregnant woman cuts your hair, it will grow faster.
- Cut your hair on a new moon to make it grow faster.
- If your eyebrows grow together, you will be very, very rich.
- If you have hairy arms, you will have a lot of money.
- A curly headed baby will be a lucky person.
- If a girl finds a hair pin or bobby pin and keeps it with her for six months without ever losing it, someone will ask her to marry by the end of that year.
- If you cut your hair and a bird weaves the fallen strands into a nest, you will go crazy.

Halloween
- It is unlucky not to provide treats for children on Halloween night when they come trick-or-treating.
- If you see a black cat on Halloween, it is very bad luck.
- If a black cat follows you on Halloween, it is really a witch in another form.
- If there is a full moon on Halloween night, don't go out at midnight or you will see demons in flight.
- If you go in a graveyard at midnight on Halloween and say, "Bloody Bones, Bloody Bones, Rise and shake," they will.
- If you kill anything on Halloween night, it will come back to haunt you.
- If you say "Bloody Mary," three times on Halloween night and look in the mirror, she will appear.

- If you say, "Bloody Mary" a hundred times on Halloween night, her whole body will appear.
- On Halloween, name an apple that hangs by a string. If you can bite it, you are beloved by the person that you have named.

hand

- If an infant clutches a coin that someone puts in its hand, it will love money when it grows up.
- If an infant does not clutch a coin that someone places in its hand, it will be a spendthrift.
- An infant that does not clutch money that is placed in its hand will grow up to be poor.
- If the hand of a newborn is closed up tight when it is born, it will be closed over savings.
- If the hand of a newborn is open when it is born, that child will grow up to be a generous giver.
- If your palm sweats, you are going to have money in your hands.
- If your palm itches, you will get money.
- If you have hairy hands, it means that money will come to you easily.

hat

- If you place a hat on someone's bed, trouble will come to the person who sleeps there.
- If you leave a hat lying on someone's bed, they may be seriously injured.
- A hat on the head will keep a child out of bed.

hay

- If you see a hay wagon passing by, make a wish and it will come true.
- Speak to your hay field and command it to yield. It will grow tall and thick.

Lonnie Boggs
Gauge, KY

healing

- The seventh son of the seventh son has the gift of healing.
- A child who has never seen their father can heal certain diseases.

hen

- If you hear a hen crow in the early part of the evening and throughout the night, you must kill it or someone will die.

hiccups

- If you get the hiccups, someone is going to tell you a story.
- If you get the hiccups and can't get rid of them, you are going to die.

hog

- To kill a hog in summer is very bad luck.

hole

- If you walk across a hole it is a good luck hole.

horoscope

- Never read your horoscope on the day of a competition or it will bring you bad luck.

horses/horse shoes

- A horseshoe brings good luck. In olden days, one was nailed above the barn door to keep the animals safe. Another was nailed over the front door of a house to bring good luck.
- A horseshoe had to be nailed so that it made a "U" shape. That was to pour the good luck in.

Seated: Sam and Amanda Blevins, holding Evie; Mary. Standing: James, Eller, and Maggie Blevins.
Clay County — Woolum, KY

- If a horseshoe was nailed upside down or accidentally got turned upside down to make the letter "n," all the good luck would run out.
- If you find a horseshoe with the toe pointed towards you, throw it over your right shoulder and make a wish.
- If you are going horseback riding, make sure you put your right foot in the stirrup first or you may have an accident before you get through with your ride.
- To find a horseshoe is a sign of good luck.
- If you find a horseshoe, spit through it, then throw it over your shoulder.

hot dog

- Eat a hot dog before a competition and it will bring you good luck.

house

- If you are playing house when you are a child and you stuff a pillow in your clothes to pretend that you are pregnant, that is the house you will be living in when you do get pregnant with your first child.

I

inchworm

- If an inchworm gets on you, he is measuring you for a new shirt.
- If you let an inch worm measure the length of your whole body, you will die. It is measuring you for a casket.

insects/bugs

- If a butterfly lands on you, like on your shirt or your jeans, it means you will be getting a new piece of clothing like the one it landed on —shirt, jeans, etc.
- A cricket on the fireplace brings good luck. Many people would keep a cricket in a small box on the mantle of the fireplace.
- If a cricket comes into your house, it is good luck if you take it back outside and don't harm it.
- If you kill a cricket in your house, bad luck will follow.

*1920 First Aid Team
Lynch, Kentucky*

- If a ladybug crawls on you, it will bring you good luck.
- If you kill a ladybug, it is bad luck for you.
- If a centipede counts your teeth, you will die.
- If a spider writes your name in its web, you will die.
- If a thousand legged worm points its legs at you, keep your mouth shut. If you let it count your teeth, they will rot out.
- If a granddaddy long legs points his legs at you, get out of his way before he puts bad luck on you.
- If you kill a spider, you will get bad news.
- If you find a granddaddy long legs in your house and choose to take it outside rather than kill it, you will have good luck.
- If you find a granddaddy long legs crawling on you and you do not harm it, it will bring you good luck.
- When the cicadas come out in full force, it is a sign that war is coming.

itching

- If your ears itch, someone is talking about you.
- If your palms itch, money will be crossing them.
- If your feet itch, you will be walking on new ground.
- If the bottom of your feet itch, you will soon be walking on strange ground.
- If your fanny itches, you are going to get a whipping.
- If your head itches, someone is coming to visit.
- If you scratch your head while thinking about something, you will forget whatever it was you were thinking of.
- If your leg itches, someone from your family it going to come for a visit and you will be amazed at how much the children have grown.

ivy

- Plant ivy around your house to keep away evil.

J

jealousy

- If you want to find out if someone is jealous, take a hair from their head and strip it between two fingernail tips. If the hair curls, the person is jealous. If it does not curl, they are not a jealous person.
- A green eyed woman will be jealous in love.

journey

- If you start on a journey and forget something important at home, you must not go back and restart your journey. Either go on without it or reschedule your journey.
- Never start a journey on Sunday.

K

kick

- Never kick a paper cup at a rodeo. If you do, you may end up getting kicked by an animal before you leave.
- To kick a dog is bad luck.
- If you kick an animal, someone will kick you before long.

kissing

- If two single people kiss under the mistletoe, they will fall in love.
- If a person kisses with their eyes open, their love is not true.

knife

- If someone hands you an open knife, hand it back to them open because if you close it before handing it back, you will bring bad luck to them.
- If you open a knife, you have to be the one to close it, or you will have bad luck.
- If someone hands you an open knife and you close it before handing it back to them, they have to make you pay them at least a dime before they take it back or bad luck will surely come to you.

- It's bad luck to give a knife away for free. Even if the other person only gives you a penny, they must give you something in return for the knife or you will both have bad luck.
- Don't give a knife to a sweetheart or your love will soon end.
- Place a knife under the bed to cut the pain of child birth in half.

knit

- If you knit a garment for someone you love, knit at least one of your hairs into the fabric and it will bind that person to you as long as they wear that garment.

L

ladder

- Standing under a ladder is bad luck.
- Crossing under a ladder is bad luck.
- If you must cross under a ladder for any reason, to reverse the bad luck, you must walk backwards under the same ladder.
- If a ladder or a staircase has thirteen or more steps on it and you step on number thirteen, you will have bad luck.

ladybug (see also **insects**)

- If an unmarried person catches a ladybug in their hands and doesn't harm it, when the ladybug flies away, it will indicate the direction from which their sweetheart will come.
- It is very bad luck to kill a ladybug.
- If a ladybug lands on you, it will bring you good luck.

laugh/laughter

- If you go to bed laughing or cutting up, someone in your family will get sick.
- If you are pregnant and you laugh and make fun of someone, your baby will have a birthmark or a defect.

leaf

- If you catch a falling leaf, you will get a letter in the mail.

- If you can catch falling leaves, you will have a pretty and happy life.

leave/leaving

- Never watch anyone leave. You may never see them again.

*Othell Vanover
McCreary
County, KY*

- If you do watch someone leave. You must always watch them leave from exactly the same spot every time.

- Always leave from the same door of the house you went in.

leg

- If your leg itches, you are going to have company that you haven't seen in a long time and you will be surprised to find how much they have grown.

leprechaun

- If you see a leprechaun, he can't leave you unless you look away.

- If you see a leprechaun, don't let him give you snuff. He'll blow it in your eyes so he can escape.

- If a leprechaun offers you more than three wishes, don't take more than three or you will lose them all.

- If you find a leprechaun's hiding place, stay away from it. If he puts the come hither on you, you'll be his slave for a thousand years.

- Leprechauns can charm animals to put the come hither on you, so stay away from your pets if they are acting very strange.

- If you see a swirl of dust, it may be a leprechaun passing by.

- Leprechauns always wear green to remind them of the country they came from—Ireland.

- Wearing green is lucky because it pleases the leprechauns to see the color of home.

- If you can keep a leprechaun with you until after dawn, he can't leave you until he grants you three wishes.

- A leprechaun has no powers during the day time.

- Wear a cross to protect you from leprechaun tricks, vampires, werewolves, witches, and any other evil thing.

lies

- If you bite your tongue, you are in the midst of telling a lie.
- If you have white specks in your fingernails, they represent recent lies you have told.
- If you bite your cheek while eating, you have been told a lie recently that you have believed.
- If your tongue turns purple, you have told a lie.
- If you are in the middle of saying something and forget what it was, it was a lie.
- If you are telling a story, get interrupted and don't ever finish the story, it was a lie.
- If you are planning on telling someone gossip that you've heard and you forget it before you see them and think of it later, it was a lie. Don't ever repeat it.

lightning

- If a leech gets on you, it won't let go until it lightnings three times.
- If a snapping turtle bites you, it won't let go until it lightnings outside.
- If a green snake bites you, it won't let go until lightning strikes.

lines

- The number of lines that are on your forehead represent the number of children you will have.
- The number of lines that are in your palm that form a clear "X" indicate the number of children you will have.
- If the lines in your right palm clearly show the letter "M," you will marry.
- If there is no "M" in the lines of your palm, you will never marry.

lip

- If your upper lip itches, you are going to be kissed by someone that is very tall.

- If your lower lip itches, you are going to be kissed by someone that is shorter than you.

love

- However many times you can pop your knuckles at one time, it represents how many people are in love with you at that time.
- If you can tie a knot in a honeysuckle vine with one hand without breaking it, the person you love will love you in return.
- On the first day of May, hold a mirror over a spring and you will see your true love reflected in the water.
- If you put your fingernail filings in a glass of lemonade and get the person you love to drink it, they will fall in love with you.
- If you bury a picture of someone you love, along with a lock of hair, they will love you in return—UNLESS someone comes along and digs the picture up. If this happens, the person will never love you.
- If you can break an apple in two with your bare hands, you will have your love returned by whomever you choose.
- If you can tie a cherry stem into a knot inside your mouth, using your tongue and teeth only, you can be assured that the person you love will fall deeply in love with you.
- If you find a tying vine and can tie it into a knot without breaking the vine, you will have the love of the one you want for your marriage partner.
- If you can peel an apple completely without breaking the peeling, let it fall on the table and the initials of the one you will marry will be spelled out of the peeling.
- If you put a drop of your blood in the coffee of your spouse without them knowing it, and they drink it, they will love you forever.
- If you have lost your boyfriend, turn his picture around in the frame so that his face is turned inward toward the back of the frame. He will come back to you.
- If you want to find out the initials of the person who truly loves you, soak your shoestrings overnight in water. The next morning, throw them on the ceiling and the wet marks they leave behind will spell out the initials of the one who loves you.

M

marriage/marry (see also **bride; wedding**)

- If the lines in the palm of your hand form an "M," this means that you will marry.
- If the first person in your family to marry has a successful and happy marriage, the rest will follow.
- If you have already set the date for your wedding, then change the date, you will not be happy in marriage.
- If you marry on a rainy day, the bride will shed that many tears during the course of her marriage.
- If you want to find out who you will marry, prepare a Dummy's Dinner. You have to do everything backwards. When the dinner is ready, whom ever comes in and sits down at the table (and is single) is the person you are going to marry.
- If you marry in white, you marry all right.
  If you marry in blue, your love will be true.
- If you can touch your index finger and your little finger behind your other fingers, you can choose whomever you want to marry.
- If a single woman accidentally knocks over a chair, she will not marry that year.
- Marry when the year is new and your love will always be faithful and true.

*Paul and Mary Belle Asher
Baxter, KY*

- If you can turn a hoe cake without breaking it, you are ready to marry.
- If you are a single woman of marrying age and the first butterfly you see in spring is white, you will soon be married.
- If you step on a cat's tail, you may never marry. If you let someone sweep under your feet without getting out of their way, you may never marry.

- If you go to a pond on the first day of spring and stare into the water, you will see the face of the man or woman you are going to marry.
- When you go to bed at night, name all four corners of your room a different person's name that you like. Whatever corner you are facing when you wake up, that name is of the person you are going to marry.
- If you accidentally turn over a chair, you will not marry that year.
- If you let someone sweep under your feet, you will not marry that year.
- If you wear red, you will never wed.
- If you find a twin berry or fruit, sleep with it under your pillow. You will dream of your husband.
- If you set your shoes on the table, you certainly will not marry that year.
- If you are the last one to marry in your circle of friends, you'll be dancing in the hog trough.
- If you sleep in a strange room, name the four corners for potential love interests. When you wake, which ever corner you are facing is the one who will return your love.
- If you get your stomach wet when you do dishes, you will marry a drunk.
- If two teaspoons wind up in the same cup by accident, there will be a marriage in the house within the year.
- If you accidentally end up with two spoons at your place at the table, you will soon be married.

matches
- It is bad luck to light two cigarettes off of one match.
- It is unlucky to strike a match for no good reason.

May
- Don't go barefoot on the first day of May or you will get sick.
- If you go barefoot on the first day of May, you will have bad luck until the next May.
- Wash your face with the morning dew from the first day of May and you will be beautiful.

- Wash your face with dew from the first day of May before sunrise and you will be lucky all the year.
- Hold a mirror over a clear running spring on the first day of May and you will see your true love's face reflected in the mirror or in the water.
- If you find a four leaf clover on the first day of May, you can marry whoever you want.

menstruating woman

- Don't let a menstruating woman bake a cake. It will fall flat.
- Don't let a menstruating woman deliver a baby.
- Don't let a menstruating woman go on any kind of game hunt.
- Don't let a menstruating woman help with home canning. The jars wont seal and the food will spoil.
- Don't let a menstruating woman plant anything in the garden. It won't grow.
- Don't let a menstruating woman walk through a garden. The plants will wither and die.

meet/meeting

- If you meet someone new, say their name out loud three times within the first few minutes of meeting them and you will remember their name.

milk

- If you spill milk, the cow that gave it will go dry.
- To spill milk is bad luck.
- To let milk boil over on the stove is bad luck.
- If you deliberately kill a frog, your cow will go dry.

mirror

- If you break a mirror, you will have seven years of bad luck.
- You must cover the mirrors in your house when someone dies for three days or you will see the departed one in the mirror.
- Never let a baby see its image in a mirror before its first birthday, or it may die.

- Mirrors attract lightning.
- Never look at yourself in the mirror by candlelight. You may see more than you want to see! (evil spirits)
- If a mirror falls off the wall for no obvious reason, there will be a death in the family.
- If you sleep with a mirror under your pillow, you will see the one you love in your dreams.
- On the first day of May, hold a mirror over a spring and you will see your true love reflected in the water.
- If you go to a clear spring of water on the first day of May, early in the morning, and hold a mirror facing over the water, you will see the face of the person you are going to marry in the mirror.
- If you let a cat see itself in a mirror, it will get jealous and bring bad luck to itself rather than to you.

mistletoe
- Hang mistletoe over your doorway during the Christmas season and you can kiss anyone who stands under it.
- Hang mistletoe over your bed on Christmas Eve and you will dream of the person you are going to marry.
- Mistletoe will protect a house from lightning.
- If a man holds mistletoe over an unmarried girl's head, he has permission to kiss her.

moles
- If you have a mole on your neck,
  you'll have money by the peck.
- Never cut or scratch the top off of a mole. It will bring bad luck.
- If a woman craves a certain food while she is pregnant and can't get it, her baby will be born with a mole in that shape.

moon
- A full moon affects the way people behave.
- More babies are born on a full moon than at any other time.

- More murders are committed on a full moon than any other time.
- More people commit suicide on a full moon than any other time.
- A man's beard grows faster on a new moon.
- Get your hair cut on a new moon, and it will grow back in faster.
- More people go crazy on a full moon than any other time.
- Never look at a new moon through the bristles of your brush.
- Never look at a new moon through bushes (shrubbery) or it will bring bad luck.
- To see a new moon in a clearing is good luck.
- If you want to insure good luck, always trim your fingernails and toenails by the light of a full moon.
- If you singe your hair on the ends at a new moon, your hair will grow more quickly.
- If you kiss the one you love under a full moon and promise to love each other forever, you will.

mouth
- If you stick a crayon in your mouth, it is bad luck.
- If someone's name comes out of your mouth by mistake, that person is thinking of you.
- A person with a weak (thin) upper lip will be weak.
- A person with two thin lips will talk too much.
- A person with a strong (big) upper lip will be brave.
- A person with balanced (proportioned) lips will be pleasant.
- A person with a small mouth will be wise.
- A person with a large, wide mouth will crave attention.

move/moving
- If you are going to move to a new house, do not take the old broom from the old house with you to the new house. It will bring bad luck.
- If you are moving to a new house, do not take your pig trough with you. It will bring bad luck.

- If you are moving to a new house it is okay to take the horseshoe over your door if you have been happy and had good luck in that house, but you must put it up over the door of the new house immediately when you get there—on the first day.

N

nails

- Never use old nails in new boards or it will bring bad luck to whatever is being built.

name

- It is good luck to name a vehicle. It will last longer. (i.e., naming a 4-wheel-drive "Bear Tracker," a car "Betsy," or naming a truck "The Silver Bullet")

neck/necklace

- If there's a mole on your neck, it means you'll have money by the peck.
- If you are wearing a necklace and the hook/latch works its way around to the front, you can make a wish before returning the clasp to the back of your neck where it belongs.
- If you wear a cream colored necklace, it will catch bad dreams and keep them away from you.
- Wearing a pearl necklace brings good luck.
- Wearing a cross necklace keeps away evil.

New Year's Eve/New Year's Day

- If you can kiss the man you love at midnight on New Year's Eve, he will be yours in the new year.
- Cook black eyed peas, greens, and ham hocks on New Year's Day and you will have good luck all year long.
- Whatever you are doing at the stroke of midnight on New Year's Eve, you will be doing the rest of the year.

Polly Asher
Leslie County, KY

- Hanging clothes on the line on New Year's Day is unlucky.
- Don't cut your hair or toenails on New Year's Day or you will have bad luck.
- When you cook greens on New Year's Day, put a Yankee Dime in the bottom of the pot. Whoever scoops out the serving that includes the dime will have good luck the rest of the year.
- Eat hog jowls on New Year's Day for good luck.
- If a man is the first person to come in your house on New Year's Day, you will have good luck.
- On New Year's morning, if a woman comes to your house first, she'll bring you bad luck.

nose
- If your nose itches, someone is coming.
- If you wear a Yankee dime around your neck, you will never have a nosebleed.
- If you have a large and well shaped nose, it means you are a friendly, nice person.

numbers
- The number 7 is lucky.
- The number of the day of your birth is lucky for you.
- Six is the number of man.
- Three is the number of perfection—the Trinity.
- The number 13 is unlucky.
- A staircase should never have 13 stairs in a row. If it is necessary, build a landing somewhere along the staircase to break it up. Otherwise the structure will always be unlucky and the people in it unhappy.
- Never stay/sleep on the 13th floor of a building.
- Friday the 13th is the most unlucky day of the year. It's best to stay home on that day if you can.
- Snake eyes (two dotted side of dice) is lucky if you roll it.
- If you walk backwards thirteen times around a grave, that person will speak to you.

- Count thirteen stars while you are lying in bed at night and then look under your bed. You'll see your coffin that you will be buried in.
- If you break anything, you'll break three.
- Bad news comes in threes.
- Death comes in threes.
- Never seat thirteen people at a table for a meal. One will die before the year is over.

O

obstacles

- If two people are walking together and they come to an obstacle, it is bad luck for them to pass on opposite sides of the obstacle.
- If two people are walking together and they come to an obstacle and go around it on different sides, they will have an argument.
- If you are walking with someone or a group and come to an obstacle, make sure all pass on the same side. If one goes the opposite way, they will have very bad luck.
- If you are walking with a friend and you come to a post, you must go around it on the same side, or you will fall out with each other. (stop being friends)

old maid

- If there is an old maid in the family, there will be one in the next generation also.

owl

- If you hear a screech owl call, it is bad luck unless you break a switch and toss it in the fire.
- If you see an owl in the middle of the day, it is a sign of bad luck coming your way.
- If you hear the screech owl call your name, don't ever answer it, no matter what or you will soon die.
- If an owl lands in the middle of your path where you are walking, turn back. It is a sign that danger lies ahead.

- If an owl lands in the road in front of your car, you must stop and go back home and cancel your journey. It is a warning to you to return home.

P

penny

- If you find a penny, pick it up, all the day you'll have good luck. Find a penny, let it lay, and bad luck will follow you the rest of the day.
- If you find a penny on heads, it will bring you good luck.
- If you see a penny on the floor or the ground and refuse to pick it up, you will have bad luck.

performance

- If a person is going to be in a play, speak in public, or sing in public, say, "Break a leg," to them before they appear for good luck.

photographs

- Don't take a picture of the dead.
- If the same person continues to show up as the middle person in a group of three, they will die before the others.
- If you burry a picture of someone you love along with a lock of their hair, they will love you in return—UNLESS someone comes along and digs the picture up. If this happens, the person will never love you.

- If the person you love leaves you, take a picture of them from the frame and face their photograph toward the back of the frame. They will never have peace until they come back to you.

Mr. & Mrs. George Vanover

pin/needle

- Find a pin, pick it up.
  All the day, you'll have good luck.
- If you hand someone a pin,
  You are sure to lose a friend.

- Before you give a pin or a needle to someone, stick it in wood first so they don't have bad luck.
- If you hand someone a pin, you are sure to lose a friend. If you are giving a pin to someone, lay it down and then let them pick it up, but it must not pass hand to hand.

pregnant (see also **baby**)

- Whatever a pregnant woman craves to eat, her baby will crave the same food as it grows up.
- If a pregnant woman makes fun of anyone with a scar, a blemish, or a deformity, she will mark her unburned baby with that same thing.
- If a pregnant woman carries the unborn child wide and all the way around her middle, it will be a girl.
- If a pregnant woman carries the unborn baby all in front like a basketball, it will be a boy.
- If a pregnant woman cuts your hair, it will grow a lot faster as her baby grows.
- If a pregnant woman is frightened severely while she's expecting, the thing that scared her will leave a mark on the unburned baby.
- This is how to determine the sex of an unborn child. Hold a needle or a pin on a piece of string over the pulse point inside your arm. If the needle swings back and forth, the baby will be a boy. If it spins or make a circle, the baby will be a girl.
- If a pregnant woman is unexpectedly frightened very badly, it is bad luck. It may make the baby come early.

Q

quarter

- If you sleep with a quarter under your pillow, it is good luck.
- If you sleep with a quarter in your pocket, it is bad luck.
- If you find a solid silver quarter, it is very good luck.
- If you place a quarter under your pillow when you go to bed and wake up to find the quarter still there, you will have good luck that day.

quilt

- Never put an unfinished quilt on a bed.
- Never sleep under an unfinished quilt!
- Sew a buckeye into a pocket in the corner of a new quilt to bring good luck. Replace it every year.
- Sew an acorn into the hem of a new quilt for good luck.

R

rabbit's foot

- If you carry a rabbit's foot in your pocket, it will bring good luck.
- If you lose a rabbit's foot, it is bad luck.
- If someone you know is having bad luck, you may trade them a rabbit's foot for any item they have in their pocket to break the bad luck.

rain

- It is bad luck to walk under a tree in the rain.

red

- It is bad luck to wear anything on your whole body that is red to a wedding.
- If your face turns red for no reason on a regular basis, you will have trouble all of your life controlling a bad temper.

red bird

- If you see a red bird and blow it a kiss, it will take the kiss to your sweetheart.
- If you see a redbird and blow it a kiss to take to your sweetheart and the redbird returns, it is bringing you love from that sweetheart.
- If a redbird lands in your path when you are walking, the next single person who crosses your path will be your true love.

remembrance

- It was good luck to chop a notch on one of the cabin logs to mark an important event when it happened.

- It is good luck to keep an item of a deceased loved one in a place of honor in our home for their remembrance. (an item like a cup, a cane, a handmade quilt, etc.)

repetition

- If you dress in the same dress three times in one day, you will have good luck.
- If you hear someone calling your name and no one is there, on the third time, stop and say, "This is _____ (Your name). What do you want?"
- If you say, "Bloody Mary," three times while looking in the mirror, you will see her ghost. Then something bad will happen.
- If you and your friend say the same thing at exactly the same time, it is a sign of true friendship and good luck for both people.
- If you and someone else say the same thing at the same time, one person can say, "jinx" on the other one (who ever says it first is the only one that counts). The person who is jinxed will have seven years bad luck if they speak a word before the sun goes down or until someone speaks their name. To release someone from a jinx, just say their name.
- If you meet someone new, say their name three times out loud, and you will never forget their name.

ring

- Never let another person take a ring off your finger. It will bring bad luck, for sure.
- If a person takes a ring off your finger to look at it, they must be the person to replace the ring back on the finger it was on.
- If you let someone else try on your engagement ring, you will not marry the person who gave the ring to you.
- You should not take off your engagement ring once it is placed on your finger until the engagement ring is replaced by a wedding band.
- If you try on someone else's engagement ring, you will bring bad luck to that person and also to yourself.
- If you drop the wedding ring during the wedding ceremony, the wedding should not be taking place.

robin

- If you make a wish when you see the first robin of springtime, that wish will come true.
- If the first robin you see in spring is flying upward, you will have good luck.
- If the first robin you see in spring is flying down to the ground, you will have bad luck.

rocking chair

- To rock an empty rocking chair is a way to invite bad luck to come in and have a seat.
- A rocking chair that rocks by itself is a sign of death coming to claim someone in that household.
- A rocking chair rocking on its own means that bad luck is coming to visit.
- If a person dies, someone else must claim a seat in that rocking chair immediately, before bad luck has a seat in it.
- If a person can rock and scoot, rock and scoot their rocking chair across the porch without getting up, they are a very lucky person.
- If a loved one is on a journey, set a pair of their old shoes in the rocking chair to bring them safely back home to their spot in the chair.

rocks

- If you find a funny looking goldish colored rock, throw it away or it will bring bad luck.
- To carry a small smooth stone in the pocket is good luck. (called a goose egg and found in a creek or stream)
- To find a rock shaped like a heart is good luck. Do not throw it away or give it away.

rooster

- If a rooster crows at midnight, it is a sign of bad luck to that household.
- If a rooster crows at your front door, it is a sign of bad luck.

- If a rooster comes and stands looking out your front door, someone new is going to be added to your family.

roots

- If you pull a vegetable out of the garden and the roots that come out with it are short or broken off, you will have bad luck.

- If you find a gen sing root in the shape of a man, it is very good luck.

David Hilton

- If you find any root in the shape of a man, it is good luck.

rose

- If you take a rose petal from a fresh rose, name it for the person you love. If you can make the rose petal pop, that person will love you in return.

- If you pick a fresh rose and the petals wilt in your hand or fall off, it is a sign that evil is close by.

S

salt

- It is bad luck to spill salt.
- If you spill salt, take a pinch and throw it over your shoulder before you clean up what has been spilled.
- If you suspect a witch has been in your house, throw salt over your left shoulder.
- It is bad luck to give salt away.
- If something has happened that you know is for sure to bring you bad luck, throw salt over your left shoulder with your right hand and it will keep the trouble from catching up with you.
- Carry a bit of salt in your pocket to keep witches away.
- If you have nightmares, put a circle of salt around the bed where you sleep and the bad dreams will have to stay away.

- If you have a stuttering problem, you can sit in front of a salt shaker and stare at it for five minutes without blinking, and the stuttering will go away.
- If someone asks you to pass the salt, do not hand it directly to them. Instead, set the shaker directly in front of them and let them pick it up.

scissors

- If you drop scissors, it means your sweetheart is cheating on you.
- Never give a gift of scissors without giving a penny with them. This insures safety for both the giver and the receiver.

scratch

- Never scratch anyone's initials into your flesh. It is very bad luck.
- If you scratch your head while you are thinking, you will forget the thing you were thinking about.
- If your head itches and you scratch it, someone you've been thinking about is coming to spend the night.
- If you scratch a green headed duck, you will have good luck.

ship

- A woman on board a ship is bad luck.
- A woman at the wheel of a ship is very bad luck.

shoes

- If you lose a shoelace (also called a shoestring), it is bad luck.
- If you lose a shoe, it is sign of bad luck coming in your life.
- If new shoes pinch your feet, someone is talking bad about you.
- If you want good luck to come to you, throw one of your shoes over your left shoulder with your right hand without looking. If it lands with the sole down, you will have good luck.
- Never walk with one shoe off and one shoe on. This invites bad luck.
- Never set a shoe(s) on the table. You will have bad luck for sure.
- If you walk with your foot partly in a shoe and walk on top of the heel, you will have bad luck.

- If you break a shoelace (shoestring) it is a sign of bad luck.
- Never put old shoelaces in new shoes.
- If your shoe accidentally comes untied and you step on your own shoestring, you are going to see the one you love.

sickness

- If a person is sick and survives the falling of leaves, they'll be around to see the leaves bud again.

sing

- It is bad luck to sing at the table.

sleep

- If you sleep on a table, it is bad luck.
- If you sleep on your back, it is bad luck.
- It is bad luck to sleep at the table.

snails/slugs

- If you sprinkle salt on a snail to watch it die, you will have bad luck.
- If you find a snail trail, look for the initials of the one you love.
- If you find a snail or a slug in the evening, don't kill it. If you spread a light layer of flour on a flat board or on the porch floor or flat railing and place the slug or snail safely there, it will write the name of the person you are going to marry in the flour. The snail or slug will be gone by morning, and the name will be left behind.
- If you sprinkle sugar on your window ceil at night before you go to bed and place a snail there also, in the morning, the snail will have written the name of the one you are going to marry.
- If you put a snail in a bag of flour and leave it overnight, by the morning, it will write the name of the one you are going to marry in the flour.

snakes

- If you kill a snake, you will get a toothache.
- If you kill a snake, you will have bad luck.

Sarah and Roy Daniel

- Garter snakes in your garden are a sign of good luck and a good crop.
- If a black snake crosses your path, you will have bad luck.
- If you try to kill a snake during the day, it won't die until the sun goes down.
- If you get bitten by a green snake, you will laugh yourself to death.
- The first thunder in a new year wakes the snakes.
- If you chase a hoop snake, it will grab its tail, make a hoop, and roll after you until it catches you.
- If you can catch a snake doctor in a jar, it is good luck. BUT once it is caught, you must let it go or you will have bad luck. (dragonfly)

sneeze

- If you sneeze on Sunday morning at the breakfast table, someone will die before the day is over.

socks

- Cowgirls often wear different color socks for good luck.
- Never wear the same socks two days in a row. Yesterday's bad luck will wear with you.

speaking

- If two people say the exact same thing at the same time, it is an opportunity for good luck. They have to lock little fingers, make a wish, and do a "pinky swear."
- If you and someone else say the same thing at the same time, one person can say, "jinx" on the other person (who ever says it first is the only one that counts). The person who is jinxed will have seven years of bad luck if they speak a word before the sun goes down or until someone speaks their name.
- To release someone from a jinx, just say their name.

spider

- To kill a spider brings bad luck.

- If a garden spider writes your name in its web, you are going to die. So, never, ever say your name in front of a garden spider.
- If a spider gets on your wedding dress, you are going to have good luck.
- Seeing a granddaddy longlegs is good luck.
- If you kill a granddaddy longlegs, you will cause it to rain.
- If you catch a granddaddy longlegs and then let him go, he will grant you one wish.
- If a granddaddy longlegs stops and looks at you and points one or two of his legs at you, he is sending you good luck.
- Never let a granddaddy long-legs count your teeth or they will rot out.
- Every time you kill a spider, you eliminate an enemy.

spilling

- Spilling salt is bad luck. To break the bad luck, take a pinch with your left hand and throw it over your left shoulder.
- Spilling milk is bad luck. The cow that gave the milk might go dry.

spit

- If you spit on a pole, you will have bad luck.
- If you spit into the wind, you will be sorry.
- If you spit on your hand before you shake hands with someone you have just made a deal with, it will seal the deal.
- If you spit on a new baseball mitt before you use it, it will bring good luck.
- If you spit in a new hat, it will bring good luck.
- If you spit at a newly married bride, it will bring her good luck.
- If you spit over a bridge into moving water, do not speak until you cross the bridge. You can make a wish and it will come true.

spoon

- If you drop a spoon, it means a woman is coming to visit.
- If you accidentally end up with two spoons at your dinner plate and you are single, it means your true love is not far away (a woman).

- If a man drops a spoon, it means an important woman in his life will visit soon.

sports

- If you compete in any kind of sporting event with change in your pocket, that is all you will win.

stars

- If you see a shooting star, make a wish right then and it will come true.
- If you see the first star appear in the night sky, you can make a wish on it and it will come true.
- If you see a blue star, it will bring you good luck.
- An animal with a star on its forehead is a lucky animal to see or own.

step/stepping

- If a staircase has many steps, it is unlucky to step on the one that is number 13 from the top or from the bottom.
- If you step over someone who is laying down, it is very bad luck.

sty

- If you meet a person with a sty, never look them in the eye, or you will surely get their sty.

sweep/sweeping

- Never let anyone sweep under your feet. If you do, you'll never marry.
- Never sweep after dark. It is bad luck.
- Never sweep out a new house with an old broom. You will bring the bad luck from the old house into the new.

T

table

- Never sit shoes on a table.
- An unmarried woman should never sit on a table or she will never marry.

teacher

- If you have mean teachers when you are in school, when you grow up, if you become a teacher, you will be mean, too.

teeth/tooth

- If you lose a tooth and don't know what happened to it, you will have bad luck.
- If you leave a newly pulled tooth under your pillow, you will have good luck.
- If you lose a tooth and a dog steps on it, the new tooth will grow in crooked.
- Cussing a lot will rot your teeth out.
- If a centipede or millipede points its legs at you, keep your mouth closed. If it counts your teeth, they will rot out.

test

- If you are having a test at school the next day, sleep with your book under your pillow. It will help you remember the answer.
- If you want to do good on a test, wear your most favorite clothes that day, fix your hair nice, and wear nice cologne. It will make you feel better and that will help you do better on the test.

thread

- If your thread tangles while you are sewing, it means your sweetheart is thinking about you.

thunder

- If you see a lightning strike, count the seconds in between it and the sound of thunder to tell you just how far away the lightning is.
- The first thunder in a new year wakes up the snakes.

toes

- If your second toe is longer than the one that is stronger, you will rule your house.

Ludley Bruce Cawood, Kentucky

189

- If a man's second toe is longer than his big toe, he will be henpecked.

tongue

- If you bite your tongue while you are talking, something you've said isn't true.
- A blister or a sore on your tongue means you have told a lie.
- If you can roll your tongue, you will have good luck.
- If you get a blister on your tongue, you have kissed a fool.
- If you bite your tongue while eating , you have recently told a lie.
- If you can flip your tongue upside down in your mouth, it means you will be a lucky person through your life.

tooth

- If you lose a tooth and a dog steps on it, the tooth will grow back in crooked.

travel

- If you start a journey and realize you have forgotten something important at home, either go on without the item or reschedule your trip. Otherwise, you as asking for bad luck.
- Never start a new journey on a Sunday.

trees

- If a willow tree shades your house, someone in the house will die.
- If you plant a cedar tree in your yard, you have to cut it down before it gets taller than the head of the house, or that person will die.

- If you stand under a pine cone tree at midnight and repeat ten times, "Red Rover, Red Rover, I dare you to come over," two wolves will appear.

tunnel

- When you pass through a tunnel, you should hold your breath going in until you come out the other side or you will have bad luck.

Oma Hilton

turtles

- If a snapping turtle bites you, it will hold on and won't let go until it thunders.
- If you find a turtle lying on its back, flip it over and it will bring you good luck.
- If you find a turtle trying to cross the road, carry it to the other side and it will bring you good luck.
- It is bad luck to see a turtle.

twins

- If one twin dies, its intelligence, essence, feelings, will be absorbed by the one that survives.
- What one twin feels, so will the other.

U

umbrella

- Opening an umbrella inside the house is inviting bad luck.
- If your umbrella turns inside out in the wind, it is a sure sign of bad luck.

V

vine

- If you find a tying vine and can tie it into a knot without breaking the vine, you will have the one you want for your marriage partner.
- If you can tie a honeysuckle vine into a knot without breaking it, you will have good luck.

W

wake

- If you go to bed at exactly 2:00 a.m. or wake at exactly 2:00 a.m., you will have very bad luck.

walk

- If you walk across a hole, it is good luck.
- If you step over a person who is lying down, it is bad luck.
- If you walk in one door of a house and walk out the other, it will bring you bad luck.
- It is bad luck to walk with one shoe off and one shoe on.
- Don't walk barefoot on the first day of May or you will get sick.
- If something bad has happened to you since you left home in the morning, walk backwards into the house when you get home. Before you can leave the house again safely, you must sit on the floor and count to ten.

water

- A ghost will not cross water.
- If you toss your dishwater out the back door and hit an elf or a leprechaun with it, you will have bad luck.

wedding

- Days of the week a marriage takes place bring certain luck.
    Monday for health,
    Tuesday for wealth,
    Wednesday best of all,
    Thursday for losses,
    Friday for crosses,
    Saturday for no luck at all.
    Sunday's mates are full of grace.
- Months of the year that a marriage takes place also bring certain luck.
    January: When the year is new, the marriage will be true.
    February: Those who wed on Valentine's Day will remain faithful, come what may.
    March: When March winds blow, they bring joy and sadness in tow.
    April: April showers bring showers of blessings.
    May: If you marry in May, you may not stay together.
    June: Happy the bride who marries in June.
    July: In July wed, you'll work for bread.

August: Those who marry in August marry in a heat of passion.

September: Marry in September, and your joy will be remembered.

October: Love will come and riches tarry.

November: Marry in November and you'll have many happy times to remember.

December: Marry in December and your love will last.

Sam Hensley and John Burton Lee

- It's bad luck for the groom to see the bride on their wedding day before the actual ceremony.

- Never let another person try on any part of your wedding clothing, veil, or jewelry that you are to be married in before the wedding. Disaster will follow before or after the wedding.

- If a single woman sleeps with a piece of a couple's wedding cake under her pillow on the night of the wedding, she will dream of who she's going to marry.

- Whoever catches the bouquet when the bride throws it after the wedding will be the next to marry.

- Whoever catches the garter when the groom tosses it out will have good luck.

- Snow on the wedding day brings money.

- On a rainy day, if a man takes a wife,
  His days will be filled with trouble and strife.
  On a sunny day if a girl weds a boy,
  Their days will be filled with laughter and joy.

- To touch a bride in her wedding gown is good luck.

- To eat a piece of the wedding cake will bring you good luck.

- If you set a wedding date, then change it, your marriage will never be a happy one.

- If a couple marries on a rainy day, the bride will shed that many tears during the course of her marriage.

- If the first butterfly you see in spring is a white one, you will soon be invited to a wedding.

Martha Hensley
Hagan, VA

- It is good luck for a bride to wear anything that belongs to you at her wedding.
- Never let anyone else try on your wedding gown before you are married. It will bring bad luck. The wedding will not take place.
- Never let another person try on your engagement ring. That person will steal your fiancé.
- Throwing rice at a wedding will bring prosperity to the bride and groom.
- For good luck, the bride should wear: something old, something new, something borrowed, something blue.
- The bride and groom must cut the first piece of wedding cake together or it is bad luck. They won't stay together if they don't cut it together.
- If anyone cuts the first piece of wedding cake before the bride and groom, the couple will always be unhappy.
- If a bride and groom jump over a broomstick together, it will bring them good luck.
- The groom carries the bride over the threshold for the first time as man and wife to insure that they will be happy together.
- The wedding ring is a symbol of eternal love. As long as the bride or groom wears their ring without taking it off, they will remain in love with their spouse.
- Anyone who kisses a new bride will have good luck.
- Thrice a bridesmaid, never a bride.
- Whichever one goes to sleep first on their wedding night—bride or groom—will be the first to die.

wetting the bed

- Playing with matches will make you wet the bed.
- Playing in fire will make you wet the bed.

wind

- If you hear the wind calling your name, do not answer. If you answer, you will die.

wishing

- Take the wishbone from a chicken or a turkey. Two people must both get hold of an end of the wishbone. On the signal, both people pull in opposite directions. The person who gets the short end will marry first. Put that piece of the wishbone over the door and whoever the first single person of the opposite sex of marrying age who walks through that door is the one you will marry.

- Take the wishbone from a chicken or a turkey and get someone else to pull it with you. Whoever pulls the long end of the wishbone gets to make a wish.

- Throw three coins in a frog pond and you may make one wish.

- Throw a coin in the water where it will never be found, make a wish, and it will come true.

- If you can blow all the seeds off of a dead dandelion in one breath, you can make a wish and it will come true.

- If you watch and count the first seven stars to appear in the night sky for seven nights in a row, then on the seventh night you may make one wish and it will come true.

witch/witches

- You can tell if someone is a witch because they will have one eye of one color and the other of another color.

- A witch will have an extra joint in a finger or be missing part of a finger.

- You can always tell a witch by an extra finger.

- You can tell a witch if you have a broom handy. If you lay a broom down across a doorway, a witch will not step over it.

- If a witch comes to your door, she will try to borrow something. Don't let her have anything and she can do you no harm.

Unidentified Volunteers
McCreary County, KY

- A witch will never let you see her in the mirror. No matter how beautiful she is on the outside, a mirror will show what she looks like under her disguise.
- If you put a pair of scissors under a chair where a witch is sitting, she cannot stand up as long as the scissors stay under her chair.
- If you have a good cow to go dry for no apparent reason, a witch might have put a spell on her.
- If a witch turns herself into an animal and you catch her and keep her in a cage until daybreak, she can never turn back into herself.
- A real witch usually has a wart on her nose or on her chin.
- A witch's eyes will glow red in the dark.
- A witch will say the Lord's Prayer backwards.
- To keep a witch out of your house, drive three nails in the shape of a triangle on your doors, or put a cross on the door.
- A horseshoe nailed over the door will keep a witch out of your house.
- Paint your doors and window ceils blue on the outside to keep a witch out of your house.

women

- A woman in a coal mine is bad luck.
- A woman at the wheel of a ship is bad luck.

wood

- Knock on wood for good luck.

*Joe, Jean, Estes, and Charles Correll
Cherokee, NC*

- If you say something has "never" happened to you, knock on wood so that it doesn't happen in the future.
- If you brag about something, knock on wood three times or you will have bad luck to pay you back for bragging.
- If you hear someone telling bad news, knock on wood three times to keep the same trouble from coming to you.
- If you speak of the dead, knock on wood to keep spirits away.
- If you tell someone something really important that you hope is going to happen to you, knock on wood to keep bad luck away.

Libby Young
Harlan, KY

Weather
Predictions

Pollyann and son, Jim Howard

Long before weather predicting became a career and an art form based on technology, people were concerned about the weather and how to prepare for it. These predictions are a result of common sense and observations handed down over the years from one generation of mountain people to another.

acorn

- If there is an abundant crop of acorns in early fall, winter will come early and be a hard one.

animal

- If woodland animals grow thicker fur than usual, it will be a cold winter.
- If outdoor animals on the farm grow thicker fur than usual, there will be a harsh winter.

ants

- If ants build their hills up high, it is going to rain.

August

- Count the fogs in August if you want to know how many snows there will be that winter.

bees

- If bees build nests in trees instead of on the ground, it will be a mild winter.
- If bees build their nests low to the ground, it will be a bad winter.

birds

- If you see a flock of birds gathered together in one place, the weather is going to turn colder.
- If birds stop singing on a summer day,
  It is a sure sign that a storm is on the way.

*Middleton and Howard Children
Baxter, KY*

- If birds wallow in the dirt, it is going to rain.
- If birds sing at dawn, it will be a clear day.
- If birds sing in the rain, it is going to rain all day.
- If you see a red bird or a blue bird sitting still in winter, it is a sign of snow on the way.

- If birds start to sing after it has been raining a while, the rain will soon stop.
- If you hear a bird singing, "Pretty bird, pretty bird," the weather will be beautiful.
- If you hear a bird singing, "Wet, wet," the weather will be rainy.
- When flocks of birds begin to fly south, cold weather is on the way.
- When flocks of birds begin to return from the south, spring is just around the corner.
- When you see a robin red breast for the first time in a new year, spring is very near.

bones

- If your bones ache, it is a sign of a change coming in the weather.
- Bones ache more in very wet weather.

cat

- If a cat sneezes, rain is on the way.
- If a cat washes his face and behind his ears, you can expect rain or snow.

chickens

- If the chickens go to roost early of an evening, it is a sign of rain before morning.
- If a chicken feeds while it's raining, it will rain all day.
- If a chicken shelters in the rain instead of eating, the rain will let up soon.
- Chickens go to roost before a storm comes.
- When hens don't lay in the winter, you know it's going to come a hard snow

chipmunk

- If a chipmunk's burrow is full of food, you can expect a bad winter.

cows

- If cows lay down under a tree, it's going to rain.

- If cows don't lay at their usual time in the field, it is going to rain or snow.
- If a cow grows a thick coat of fur, it is going to be a bad winter.

clouds

- If it clouds up on a frost, it means snow is on the way.
- If clouds are golden colored in the evening, it means the weather the next day will be fair.

dawn

- Grey skies in the morn, sailor be warned. (bad weather coming that day)
- Red sky in the morning, sailor take warning. (bad weather is coming that day)
- Red sky in the morning, shepherd take warning. (bad weather is imminent)
- Red skies at break of day mean bad weather is on the way.

deer

- When you hear the deer blow, there will soon be snow.

dog

- If a dog lays on the porch with no one around and begins to wag his tail for no reason, it is a sign of rain coming.

Easter

- If there is an early Easter, there will be an early spring.
- If there is a late Easter, there will be a late spring.
- If it rains on Easter Sunday, it will rain the next four Sundays.

fire

- If you build a fire outside in the winter and it pops as it burns, you will have new snow within three days.
- If you build a fire in the fireplace and it makes a hissing sound, you can be sure the weather will be wet. If it pops and cracks, weather will be dry.

fish

- If fish break the water and jump out, rain is coming.

flies

- When flies swarm, rain is on the way.
- When flies bite, it is going to storm.

Doug and Sarah Boggs
Hickman Hill, Stearns, KY

fog

- When fog comes out in narrow little puffs from the mountains, foes are brewing their coffee and waiting for the weather to clear.
- For every fog there is in August, the will be a snow in winter.
- Heavy fogs in June or July mean it will be an early winter.
- Ever how many foggy days there are in August, there will be an equally snowy day in winter.
- If it's foggy before seven, the sun will shine before eleven.
- If you wake up to a foggy morning, it will be a warm day and the sun will shine by noon.
- If heavy fog settles in before nightfall and lingers until 11:00 p.m. on any of the first ten days of January, the winter will be worse than anticipated.
- If fog lingers late in the morning, the day will be bright and sunny.
- If it is raining and the fog starts to rise on the mountains, the rain will soon stop.

food

- When all the food on the table is eaten, it will be dry the next day.

fox

- If a fox makes its hole deep in the ground, it will be a hard winter.

frogs

- If you hear frogs chirping in the middle of the day, it is a sure sign that rain is on the way.

- If frogs begin to holler in March or April, they will soon be looking through glass windows. (It will be cold enough for water to freeze on top again before warm weather stays.)
- If you find frogs deep in a mine, it will be a bad winter.
- If frogs holler early in the day, you know it is going to rain.
- If you hear a tree frog chirping, rain is not far off.

frost

- For every frost there is in September, there will be a snow in winter.
- For every frost there is in August, there will be an equal number of snows in winter.
- If there are a lot of frost worms crawling around in the fall, it will be a bad winter.
- Two frosts in a row followed by a lot of rainy days means cold weather is near.
- If frost hangs on the timber late in the morning, you will know snow is coming.

general

- If you want to know what the next twelve months of weather will be like, record what the weather is like each day for the first twelve days of weather after Christmas.
- If a cricket chirps, the weather will rise.

groundhog

- If the groundhog sees his shadow when it comes out of the den in spring and runs back into the den, there will be six more weeks of bad weather.
- If the groundhog does not see his shadow and stays out of his den for a little while on the first day he comes out of the den, spring is just around the corner.
- Some people say that February 2nd is Groundhog Day, but the groundhogs don't always know that.

hair

- If you have natural curly hair and the curls tighten up, it is surely going to rain.

- If you have naturally fuzzy hair and it gets fuzzier, it is a sign of rain on the way.
- If you have a perm and your hair frizzes up, it is going to rain.
- If you curl straight hair and the curls fall out as soon as you take it down, it is going to rain.
- When you comb your hair in winter and find it full of static electricity, the weather will be cold and clear.

horse

- A horse in an open field will run and whinny before a storm arrives.

insects

- If there are a lot of black bugs crawling about in the fall, there will be many snows in winter.
- If butterflies disappear early in the fall, it will be a bad winter.
- If insects are still flying about in November, it will be a cold hard winter.
- If hornets build their nests low to the ground, it means a bad winter lies ahead.
- If hornets build nests in the tops of the trees, winter will be mild.
- If you see yellow butterflies in fall, the leaves will turn to match.
- Watch for the appearance of yellow butterflies to appear in the fall. Ten days later there will be a frost, causing the leaves to change and match the color of those butterflies.
- If you see any insect carrying material to make a bed, be sure that cold weather is not far ahead.

January

- If you watch the first twelve days of January, they will foretell the next twelve months' weather.
- Count the days of fog in January and you may expect that many frosts in May.

July

- If it rains on the first day of July, the whole month will be rainy.

June

- If it rains on the first day of June, it will be rainy all summer.

leaves

- If leaves turn their bottom sides up, it is going to rain.

lightning

- Lightning in the north is a sign of dry weather.

March

- If snow falls on the first day of March, it will snow all month.
- If March comes in like a lion, it will go out like a lamb.
- If March comes in like a lamb, it will go out like a lion.

moon

- If the moon has a ring around it, count the stars inside the ring and you will know how many days there will be of clear weather ahead.
- However many days old the moon is on the first snow tells how many snows there will be during that winter.
- It will rain within three days if the horns of the moon point down.
- If the moon has two rings around it, it will snow within twenty-four hours.
- If the weather is clear on a new moon, it will be fair with the next change of the moon.

night

- If the weather clears in the night and becomes fair, the fair weather will not last long.

owl

- The weather will be fair and clear if you hear a screech owl.

pain

- A person with arthritis is a good weather predictor. If their arthritic joints hurt, the weather is going to change to either rain or snow.

pine cones

- If there are a lot of pine cones on the ground in the fall, there will be a lot of snow in the winter.

rabbit

- If you keep a rabbit in a cage, it will bounce around before rain or snow comes.

rain/raindrops

- If it rains in the sunshine, it will rain again at the same time tomorrow.
- Rain before seven will stop before eleven.
- Good Friday brings bad weather.
- If a cat sneezes, you may expect it to rain before the day is over.
- When raindrops bead up on leaves, there is more rain to come.
- If it rains on the first Sunday of the month, it will rain every Sunday of that month.
- If birds sing in the rain, it is going to rain all day.
- If a flock of birds gathers together in one place, it is going to rain or storm.
- If cows graze in the rain, the rain will not last long.
- If cows huddle in the rain, it will be a heavy rain.
- If it rains on Easter Sunday, it will rain the following seven Sundays in a row.
- If it rains on any change of the moon, it will rain until the next chain of the room.
- If raindrops cling to tree leaves, the rain is not over.
- Large raindrops are a sign of a short rain.
- Rain will usually let up in time to milk the cows.
- April showers bring May flowers.

Pansy Post Office and Store — 1903

- If chickens take shelter in the rain, it will soon stop.
- If chickens stay out in the rain, it will rain all day.
- There is a little bird that says, "wet, sure . . . wet, wet, sure . . . " If you hear it, you can count on rain 2–4 hours later.
- If leaves show their back side up, it is going to rain.
- A cow lifting its tail without using the bathroom is a sign that rain is coming.
- If you hear a rain crow cawing, rain is on the way.
- If you wash your car, it is sure to rain.
- If bubbles stand in a mud puddle after it rains, there will be rain again the same time tomorrow.

rainbow
- A rainbow in the west is a sign of wet weather to come.
- A rainbow in the east is a sign of dry weather to come.
- If you see a rainbow, there will be no more rain that day.

red
- Red sky in the morning, sailor take warning.
  Red sky at night, sailor's delight.
- Red sky in the morning, shepherds take warning.
  Red sky at night, your sheep will sleep tight.

rooster
- If a rooster crows at midnight, bad weather is approaching.
- When skeeter legs grow and roosters crow, spring is here.
- If in winter the roosters crow, you will know to expect snow!

seasons
- The first three days in any season are an indication of what weather will be like during that season.

sky (see also **dawn**)
- A green sky is a sure sign of severe weather including hail or a tornado.
- A salmon sky is a sign of good weather.

- A mackerel sky is a sign of bad weather.
- Red sky at night, sailors' delight.
- A red sky at night is a shepherd's delight.
- Red sky at night, the devil is beating his wife.

smoke

- It will be fair weather if smoke rises.
- If smoke goes down toward the ground, expect rain.
- When smoke from a chimney settles to the ground, there is going to be bad weather.
- When the smoke from the chimney rises straight up, the weather will be clear and cold.
- When the smoke from the chimney drifts to one side or the other in a curve, then straight out, there is a change coming in the weather.

snow

- Heavy, deep foliage in summer is a sign of deep snows in winter.
- However many days old the moon is on the first snow tells how many snows there will be during that winter.
- Count the number of days from the date of the first snow until Christmas and you will find the number of snows that will fall that winter.
- If snow lies on the mountains, there's more to come.
- If snow lies on the mountains, it is laying for another one.

spiders

- If there are many spiders moving about in the fall, the winter will be a bad one.
- If you kill a granddaddy long -legs, it will rain.
- If you see that spiders have built their webs in the grass or in bushes low to the ground, you can expect rain the following day.

spring

- You know spring is not really here until the oak trees let loose of their leaves. (begin to bud)

- A very rainy spring usually means a very dry summer.
- When you see the first Robin Red Breast, you'll know that spring is near.
- Spring will not be complete until you have seen the following winters in this order:

    Sarvice Winter: These are the first white buds to come out in the mountains.

    Redbud Winter: These are the little purple blooms on low growing trees along roadways and other lower places.

    Dogwood Winter: These are the large white blossoms in the shape of a cross that grow abundantly throughout the mountains.

    Blackberry Winter: When blackberry briars are full of white blossoms, you will know that the last of cold weather is close at hand.

squirrels

- If a squirrel starts gathering nuts earlier than usual, the winter will be a bad one.
- If a squirrel's tail is bushier than usual, it will be a cold winter.
- If a squirrel's fur is unusually thick, it is putting on a winter coat for freezing weather ahead in the winter.

sun

- If the sun has a haze around it, there is going to be a long dry spell.
- If the sun comes out right after a short rain, it will rain again the same time the next day.

thunder

- If there is rumbling thunder in the fall, it is going to be a bad winter.
- If it thunders in the winter, very cold weather will follow.
- If it thunders in January, it is going to be a wet spring and a hot summer.
- If it thunders in January, it will frost in May.
- A holly berry tree planted near your house will keep away lightning and thunder.

- If it thunders in February, there will be frost in May on about that same day.
- The first thunderstorm in the spring wakes up the snakes, and there will be no more harsh winter left after that.

trees

- If fruit trees produce bumper crops, it is going to be a harsh winter.
- If nut bearing, or cone bearing trees produce more than usual, there is a difficult winter ahead.
- If berry bearing plants, briars, bushes, and trees, produce a large crop, it is going to be a cold, bad winter.
- If there are a lot of blooms on the locust tree, summer will be mild.

turkeys

- If turkeys go to roost early of an evening, it is a sign that rain is on the way.

wind

- Lick your finger and hold it straight up in the air to see which direction the wind is blowing.
- A dry wind in June means no blackberries in July.
- Pick a few blades of grass and lay them on your hand to see which way the wind is blowing.
- Wind from the north brings cooler weather.
- Wind from the south brings warmer weather.
- Wind from the west brings a change in weather.
- Wind from the east means the weather you just had is going to double back in on you and repeat itself.

window

- If you can see the sun's reflection in the window as it goes down, the next day will be a very pretty day.
- Frost gathered in the corner of a window pane means a cold snap.
- Frost filling the bottom half of a window pane means a cold spell.

- Frost filling window panes means bad weather is going to hold on a while.

winter

- Heavy deep foliage in summer is a sign of deep snow in winter.
- If birds eat all the pokeberries from the stalk, it will be a rough winter.
- You can gage a winter by how thick (plentiful) the forage (nuts) is.
- If the fuzzy caterpillars come out in summer, it will be a hard, long, bad winter.
- If it is warm in winter, it will be cold the following spring.
- It will be a cold, long winter if squirrels start gathering nuts in September.
- If the north side of a beaver's dam is thicker, it is going to be a cold winter.
- If hornets build their nests in bushes, there will be a bad winter.
- If a squirrel's tail is bushier than usual, look out for a cold winter.
- If birds huddle on the ground in the fall, it is going to be a bad winter.
- If hornets build their nests closer to the ground than usual, it is going to be a bad winter.
- If hornets' nests are thicker, with more layers on them than usual, it is going to be a bad winter.
- If crickets stay in the chimney in the fall, it is going to be a hard winter.
- If the wooly worms are solid black, the next season is going to be a bad one.
- If there is a big crop of berries and nuts in the bearing months, the winter that follows will be a hard one.
- If the laurel bush's leaves roll up in summer, a cold winter is on the way.
- If the wooly worms begin to crawl before the first frost, it is going to be a bad winter.
- If the sweet potatoes are harder than usual, there is a bad winter to follow.

- If the corn shucks are thicker than normal, a bad winter is on the way.
- A cold winter will be followed by a hot summer.

worms/wooly worms

- If a lot of worms come out of the ground, a heavy rain will soon follow.
- If the wooly worm is black it will be a bad winter.
- If the wooly worm is orange, it will be a mild winter.
- If the wooly worm is orange in the middle and black on both tips, the winter will start out bad, get better, and go out with a bang.
- If the wooly worm is orange on both ends and black only in the middle, there will be a bad spell in the middle of the winter.

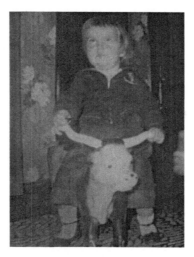

Judy Hensley

MOUNTAIN WISDOM: *Mountain Folk, Volume 1* readers, for
other Little Creek Books titles you may enjoy, or to purchase
additional copies of MOUNTAIN WISDOM: *Mountain
Folk, Volume 1*, signed by the author, visit our website:

www.littlecreekbooks.com

If you enjoy reading books like **MOUNTAIN WISDOM:** *Mountain Folk,* **Volume 1**, *you will also want to read these Little Creek Books titles:*

IN THE GARDEN WITH BILLY:
Lessons About Life, Love and Tomatoes
Renea Winchester

One woman: far from home and struggling to accept her mother's terminal illness. **One man:** recently widowed, and maintaining the old ways of farming; while being surrounded by urban sprawl. One story: about what happens when a harried suburban mom reaches out to help a stranger. A chance encounter on a busy Atlanta summer day turns into an unexpected friendship for Renea Winchester. She's in a hurry, running to her daughter's tennis lesson and away from the reality of her mother's illness when her daughter notices a primitive sign on the side of the road which reads, "Baby Goats 4 Sale." Even though Renea has no interest in smelling goats, she pulls into the drive on that hot day and meets a man who would change her life. Wearing faded cotton overalls, and walking with a slight stoop, seventy-seven year old Billy Albertson shakes Renea's hand and captures her heart. Join these unusual friends in the garden as they lean on each other, push through obstacles, and face life's challenges with integrity and hope.

EATING LOCAL IN VIRGINIA
Phyllis Wilson

"Christ talked about the vine and the vineyard, the fisherman and the good shepherd. He made farming sound like a process, almost like religion. Virginia is a state that is biblical in its proportions — it has vineyards and orchards; streams with native trout and a long Atlantic coastline; open fields for grazing and woodland habitat for deer and small game."

Thus begins EATING LOCAL IN VIRGINIA, the ultimate guide to local foods in Virginia. Phyllis Wilson has compiled it all in one smart reference. Whether you are wondering where to buy the freshest vegetables or meat raised in a humane fashion without steroids and hormones you will find it all in EATING LOCAL IN VIRGINIA. Farms open to the public, farm stores, farmers' markets, as well as stores and restaurants who seek out locally raised food are all listed here.

Wilson believes that people are beginning to wake up and realize the inherent problems in our grain-based factory food system and the damage it is doing to our health. She sees the local food movement as people reaching out to a better system. But where does one find good naturally grown food? Often, this becomes a problem.

In her book she takes the reader on a journey across the state visiting farms and restaurants, asking the right questions, and listening to the comments of the people who raise our food. Join her on the journey and you will never again have to ask "what shall we eat?" or "where shall we dine?"

To read works written by the talented women who
call Appalachia "home," visit

www.mountaingirlpress.com

The stories depicted in THE ZINNIA TALES, SELF-RISING FLOWERS and CHRISTMAS BLOOMS, will take you to a place where strong women survive. Each short story collection is filled with stories that celebrate what it means to be an "Appalachian woman." Each collection will strike a note with anyone who has ever called the mountains home, or just wishes she lives there. Readers will delight in the warmth of these tales which demonstrate the richness of the place where these women live their lives, and tell their stories. Fiction about women, written by women, these works exemplify the Mountain Girl Press mission statement: Stories that celebrate the wit, humor and strength of Appalachian women.

Coming in 2011

MOUNTAIN WISDOM
Mountain Folk
Volume 2

Mountain people use beautifully poetic language that includes similes, metaphors, idioms, and euphemisms to color every day speech. Mountain language is more than dialect or accent. It is a lyrical embodiment of common sense, observations, humor, and emotions. MOUNTAIN WISDOM: *Mountain Folk, Volume 2* is filled with examples of what makes mountain language so unique. Make sure to check www.littlecreekbooks.com for details on the release of MOUNTAIN WISDOM: *Mountain Folk, Volume 2* in 2011.

Breinigsville, PA USA
08 November 2010
248849BV00003B/7/P